# In Search of the Christian Buddha

# In Search of
# the Christian Buddha

*How an Asian Sage
Became a Medieval Saint*

## Donald S. Lopez Jr.
*and* Peggy McCracken

W. W. NORTON & COMPANY

NEW YORK | LONDON

For information about permission to reproduce selections from this book,
write to Permissions, W. W. Norton & Company, Inc.,
500 Fifth Avenue, New York, NY 10110

For information about special discounts for bulk
purchases, please contact W. W. Norton Special Sales at
specialsales@wwnorton.com or 800-233-4830

Manufacturing by Courier Westford
Book design by Fearn de Vicq
Production manager: Louise Parasmo

ISBN 978-0-393-08915-8

W. W. Norton & Company, Inc.
500 Fifth Avenue, New York, N.Y. 10110
www.wwnorton.com

W. W. Norton & Company Ltd.
Castle House, 75/76 Wells Street, London W1T 3QT

1 2 3 4 5 6 7 8 9 0

# Contents

# In Search of the Christian Buddha

# Introduction

"He was a son, as they say, of a great king both rich and powerful." So begins Marco Polo's account of the life of the Buddha, dictated to Rustichello da Pisa, a writer of romances, when the two men shared a prison cell in Genoa in 1298. Seven years earlier Polo had returned to Italy after two decades of travels through Asia. In the *Description of the World*, as the earliest version of Polo's account is known, the Venetian traveler does not use the name "Buddha." He speaks instead of an idol called Sagamoni Borcan, a name he likely learned at the pleasure dome of Kublai Khan in Xanadu. Sagamoni is Mongolian for Śākyamuni, "sage of the Śākya clan" in Sanskrit. Borcan is the Mongolian word for Buddha.

Polo's account of the Buddha includes the story of the prince's youth, his father's attempt to isolate him from the ills of the world, his discovery of old age and death despite the king's efforts to protect him from knowledge of them, and his turn away from his father's worldly kingdom to seek a spiritual realm. The description of Sagamoni Borcan concludes with these words: "And they do hold him for the greatest of all their gods. And they tell that the aforesaid image of him was the first idol that the Idolaters ever had; and from it have originated all the other idols. And this happened in the Island of Seilan in India. The Idolaters come there on pilgrimage from very great distances and with great devotion, just as Christians go to the shrine of Saint James in Galicia."[1]

Polo tells the story of the Buddha from a Christian perspective and compares a Buddhist pilgrimage site to the most famous pilgrimage site in all of Europe, Santiago de Compostela. For the Venetian, the Buddha was saintly: "And there he abided, leading a life of great hardship and sanctity, and keeping great abstinence, just as if he had been a Christian. Indeed, had he but been so, he would have been a great saint of Our Lord Jesus Christ, so good and pure was the life he led."[2] This positive portrayal of the Buddha is extraordinary for its time. In the long history of contact between Christians and Buddhists, Christians would far more often condemn the Buddha as an idol and a purveyor of idolatry than revere him as a saint.

There are dozens of manuscript versions of Marco Polo's *Description of the World*, and many translations of his book were made soon after it was written. In one copy from 1446, right after the passage about Saint James, an unknown scribe added a comment: "This is like the life of Saint Iosafat who was the son of the king Avenir of those parts of India, and was converted to the Christian faith by the means of Barlaam, according as is read in the life and legend of the holy fathers."

This Iosafat, or Josaphat, was so well known in the Middle Ages that a copyist could allude to his similarity to Sagamoni Borcan in passing. Ours is a book about this seeming similarity. It seeks to answer this question: How did the Buddha become a Christian saint?

The earliest known version of the legend of the Christian saint Josaphat and his teacher, Saint Barlaam, appears in the Georgian language in the ninth or tenth century CE and is based on an Arabic story that is, in turn, based on the life of the Buddha. The Georgian text was translated into Greek, then into Latin, and then into virtually every language spoken in Europe during the Middle Ages. It made its way to Asia in 1591 through a Japanese translation, and in 1712 to the Philippines in Tagalog. The account of the Christian Indian prince was made into plays, including the fifteenth-century French *Mystère du roy Avenir*, attributed to Jean de Prieur, and *Barlaán y Josafat*, written in 1611 by Lope de Vega, the most important dramatist of the Spanish Golden Age. Some of the narrative would be appropriated by later writers: the story of the Three Caskets, well known from *The Merchant of Venice* (and later the subject of an essay by Freud) comes from *Barlaam and Josaphat*. The legend also inspired devotion to its protagonists. In 1571, the Doge of Venice presented a bone from Josaphat's spine to King Sebastian of Portugal; in 1672, the relic was enshrined in Saint Andrieskerk in Antwerp. A church with the dedication "Divo Josaphat" inscribed over the entrance was built in Palermo in the sixteenth century. In 1583, Pope Sixtus V authorized November 27 as the feast day of Saints Barlaam and Josaphat; the Eastern Orthodox Church assigned August

26 as Josaphat's feast day and the Georgian Orthodox Church chose May 19.

There are many reasons for the legend's great popularity, and we will discuss them in the pages that follow. But, put most simply, *Barlaam and Josaphat* is a story about how to lead our lives. Should we live in the world—a world of joy and sorrow—or should we renounce it in order to find a better world in the life to come? This is a perennial question, pondered over the millennia by philosophers and saints from around the world. In some sense, it is the most basic question: If life ends in death, how should I live?

After the passing remark of Marco Polo's editor, the fact that the life of the Buddha resembled the story of Barlaam and Josaphat would go largely unnoticed until 1859, four hundred years later. By that time, the obscure Asian idol had become the famed Buddha, the founder of a great religion, and a figure revered by many in the Victorian Age not for his sanctity but for his humanity, and for teaching the path to salvation to all social classes without the need for priests or rituals, or even the need for God. By that time, Josaphat was largely forgotten. And so in the nineteenth century, it was not that the life of the Buddha was like *Barlaam and Josaphat*; *Barlaam and Josaphat* was like the life of the Buddha. The order, and the priority, had been reversed.

In a sense, the legend put Buddhism and Christianity in dialogue for centuries, without the interlocutors recognizing each other. And before *Barlaam and Josaphat* became a Christian story, it took its most enduring shape as the Arabic work *Bilawhar and Būdhāsaf.* Over the course of its evolution, the legend put Muslims, Jews, and Christians into contact, again, without mutual recognition. Although we will have much to say about Buddhism, Christianity, and Islam in the pages that follow, our focus will be on the story and its translations. Following in the steps of previous scholars, we will trace the circuitous pilgrimage of the story as it moves from Buddhist to Muslim and, finally, to Christian worlds. Our task, then, will be to ask not how stories circulate among religions, but how religions circulate among stories.

# CHAPTER ONE

# The Storied Buddha: The Indian Tale

Since the nineteenth century, the Christian story of *Barlaam and Josaphat* has been invariably linked to the life of the Buddha. Some scholars have gone so far as to call it "a Buddhist tale." We will consider how Buddhist it is in the chapters that follow, but we need first to begin with the story of the Buddha as it has been told in Asia.

There is general agreement that the Buddha was a historical figure, the most successful of a group of itinerant teachers in northern India between 600 and 400 BCE. However, the Buddha's teachings were not written down until centuries after his death, and the first biographies not until the first centuries of the Common Era. It is thus hard to verify the facts in those biographies with a high degree of certainty. The traditional account of his final days says that he lived for eighty years, and that number is generally accepted. However, there is considerable disagreement over the question of when those eighty years began and ended. For the Buddhist traditions of South-east Asia, the Buddha died in 544 BCE. Some scholars have placed his death as late as 380 BCE.

Our focus, however, is not the actual life of the Buddha but the story told about him. There are many accounts, from many periods of history and from many lands. They do not agree in every detail. Sometimes they differ on a particular event or on the protagonists in a particular scene. Some accounts are much more elaborate than others, adding events and expanding on standard elements of the story.[1] Here, we provide a composite version of the Buddha's life, focusing on the most common elements.

The life of the Buddha does not begin with the birth of a baby, but with the birth of a vow: to become a Buddha and to free all beings from suffering. Central to Buddhism is the doctrine of rebirth, that all beings in the universe have been reborn billions of times in the past, without beginning. At particular moments in the history of the universe, particularly compassionate humans have made the remarkable promise to free their fellow creatures from the cycle of birth and death by seeking a state of perfection called Buddhahood. It takes eons for the person who has made the promise (called a *bodhisattva*) to accumulate the good deeds that will eventually fructify in enlightenment. Traditionally, the virtues of the bodhisattva are either six (giving, ethics, patience, effort, concentration, wisdom) or ten (giving, ethics, renunciation, wisdom, effort, patience, truthfulness, determination, loving-kindness, and equanimity). The bodhisattva cultivates limitless variations of these virtues over billions of lifetimes in a variety of forms:

male, female, human, animal, or god. (There are six realms of rebirth in the Buddhist cosmos: those of gods, demigods, humans, animals, ghosts, and denizens of various hells.)

And so the story of the Buddha dwells at length on his previous lives, and on the Buddhas who preceded him. Three, six, and twenty-four have all been given as the number of Buddhas who preceded the Buddha of our story. There are two reasons why the stories of his previous lives are told and retold. First, they show how difficult it is achieve the exalted rank of a Buddha. And second, they demonstrate that the Buddha was not an ordinary man.

The Buddha's chief rivals, and sometimes actual antagonists, were Brahmin priests, who performed sacrifices in order to win boons from the gods for their patrons. These sacrifices were prescribed in the Vedas, ancient texts that scholars date as far back as 1700 BCE. But within the Hindu tradition itself the Vedas are said to be timeless, having existed forever in the form of sound. They were heard by ancient sages and then passed down orally over generations. In one sense, it is inappropriate to call them "scriptures" or "texts" because they were not written down for centuries; the oldest extant manuscript dates only from 1464. These most sacred of Hindu scriptures are called *śruti*, "that which is heard."

In such a setting, any new religion that challenges the authority of these ancient teachings must account for its own origins and must produce an equally venerable pedigree. This was clearly a problem for early Buddhism. It could not simply claim that a prince sat down under a tree one night and discovered the meaning of the universe. Regardless of the profundity of his insight, what authority would such a claim carry? Therefore, we see in early Buddhism a strong emphasis on the past. The Buddha, it was said, did not simply arrive at his insight on his thirty-fifth birthday. In fact, he had taken a vow to become a Buddha billions of years earlier and had been perfecting himself over billions of lifetimes in order to finally see the truth that night. Furthermore, he was not the first Buddha; there had been many Buddhas in the past, each of whom had understood the same reality, each of whom had taught the same *dharma*, the same truth. But if this was the case, why was there no record or memory of them? Because, it was said, there was no reason for a new Buddha to appear in the world until all the teachings of the last Buddha had been forgotten and had completely disappeared from the world. Their existence was revealed anew by a new Buddha, who had complete memory of the past. Indeed, it was said that on the night of his enlightenment, the Buddha had a vision of all of his past lives, including his memories of the previous Buddhas. Meditating all night, at dawn he became a Buddha himself, and over the course of his life he taught the same truths that the previous Buddhas had taught.

And so the life story of the Buddha is the story of many lives. Over five hundred *jātaka* ("birth") tales recount stories of the Buddha's previous lives as a fish, a deer, a rabbit, a monkey, and, often, a king. Even an account of the lifetime in which the bodhisattva became the Buddha must begin in the immediately previous life.

## The Birth of the Buddha

In Buddhism, there is no single, eternal God. Instead there are many gods, beings who through their virtuous deeds in the past are reborn—for long but finite lives—in one of a number of heavens. In his penultimate lifetime, the bodhisattva was such a god in the Joyous Heaven. After so many lifetimes on the path to enlightenment, he had gained the ability to choose the circumstances of his final rebirth. From heaven he surveyed the earth and decided the place and time; he chose his clan (Śākya) and his caste (warrior). He chose his parents, King Śuddhodana and Queen Māyā of the city of Kapilavastu, near the foothills of the Himalayas in what is today southern Nepal. His mother dreamed that a six-tusked white elephant— an auspicious symbol of royal sovereignty—had entered her womb, and she knew she was with child. Queen Māyā's pregnancy is described as blissful and her womb is described as a sumptuous palace for the future Buddha, who sits cross-legged there. After the usual ten lunar months, as his mother is walking in a garden, he emerges from her right side without causing her the slightest pain. The child is caught on a golden net held by four gods, and two streams of water, one warm and one cold, descend from the heavens to wash him—although he has emerged from the womb free from all impurity. The child can immediately walk and talk. He looks in all directions and then takes seven steps to the north, a lotus blossoming under his feet at each step. He points with his right hand to heaven and with his left hand to earth and declares, "Chief am I in all the world. Eldest am I in all the world. This is my last birth. No more will

I be reborn." Many miracles attend his birth. The earth shakes, a brilliant light suffuses the world, the blind see, the deaf hear, the lame walk, the fires of hell are extinguished, trees bear perfect flowers and fruit, and the salty sea turns sweet.

The child is presented to his father, who summons the astrologers and seers to examine the prince and prophesy his destiny. All but one of them hold up two fingers: If the child remains in the world, he will become a great ruler. However, if the child renounces the world, he will become a Buddha. One of the seers holds up only one finger, saying that there is no doubt: the child will become a Buddha.

The king names his son Siddhārtha, "he who fulfills his goal." Seven days after her child's birth, Queen Māyā dies. Different versions of the tale give various reasons for the queen's death. One explains that she died of joy at the birth of her wondrous child. Another says that had she lived until her son renounced the world, she would have died of a broken heart on that day. It is also said that after a Buddha has occupied a woman's womb, no other being may enter there, and so she must die seven days after his birth. The king chooses another of his wives, Queen Māyā's sister, to raise his infant son.

The father then brings the infant prince to the temple, where the statues of the gods rise from their pedestals and fall prostrate at his feet. The king also bows before his son, calling him *devātideva*, "god beyond the gods." Fearing that the prince will be exposed to the sorrows of the world and renounce it to become a mendicant, as the royal seers predicted he might, the king sequesters him in a palace, where he is surrounded only by the young, the healthy, and the beautiful. Thus, Prince

Siddhārtha remains unaware of aging, sickness, and death. He excels at all the arts and sciences, including the manly arts of sport and war. He strings a great bow that no other man can master and shoots an arrow with such force that it penetrates the earth and creates a spring. His virile virtue wins him the hand of a beautiful maiden named Yaśodharā, and at the age of twenty-nine, after his marriage and (according to most accounts) the birth of his son Rāhula, Prince Siddhārtha decides to leave the palace to seek a state beyond suffering.

## The Four Sights

There are significant variations among the descriptions of the prince's decision to leave his life of worldly pleasures. In a work called *The Noble Search* (*Ariyapariyesanā*), the Buddha's account of his decision is brief: "Later, while still young, a black-haired young man endowed with the blessing of youth, in the prime of life, though my mother and father wished otherwise and wept with tearful faces, I shaved off my hair and beard, put on the yellow robe, and went forth from the home life into homelessness."[2] This single sentence is the only description of the Buddha's renunciation of the world. However, the better-known account of the prince's decision to abandon worldly attachments is more elaborate and begins with an account of his famous four chariot rides outside the palace.

At the request of Prince Siddhārtha, who has become curious about the outside world, the king reluctantly agrees to allow his son to ride outside the gates of the palace. However, unbeknownst to his son, he makes careful preparations for the outing, selecting the route, stationing musicians in the trees, carpeting the road with flowers, and, most importantly, removing any aged, lame, or sick people from his son's path, since in his twenty-nine years the prince has never seen infirmity or witnessed misfortune.

The prince's excursions have something of the quality of the *rathayātrā* (literally, "chariot procession"), an ancient Indian tradition in which the statue of a deity is taken from the temple and wheeled in a chariot along a prescribed route. The purpose of the procession is to provide *darśana*, or "seeing," the opportunity for the devotee to see the deity and receive its blessing. Royal processions serve a similar function. The difference in the case of Prince Siddhārtha, however, is that instead of being seen, he sees, and the four sights, as they are called, provide one of the pivotal moments in his biography. In the most detailed version of the story, the prince takes four chariot rides outside the city, and, in each case, departs from a different gate of the palace: east, south, west, and north.

Despite the best efforts of the king, on the first excursion an old man—white-haired, toothless, supported by a staff, his body bent and shaking—somehow appears along the prince's route. Some accounts ascribe the old man's presence to chance; others say that the gods placed him there. Never having seen such a thing before, the prince stops and asks his charioteer what he sees before him. His charioteer tells him that he sees an old man. The prince then asks whether this is *the* old man, the only one in the world, or whether there are others like him. His charioteer explains that there are many like him, and that old age will come to all humans, including his father the king and the prince himself. Dumbstruck at the revelation, Prince Siddhārtha instructs his charioteer to return to the palace. Later he ventures forth a second time and encounters a sick man. Again learning that this fate will come to all, he returns despondently to the palace. On the third excursion, the prince encounters death for the first time. Sons are carrying the corpse of their father to the charnel ground. The widow and daughters follow, weeping in the corpse's wake. When the prince's charioteer explains what the sons bear on their shoulders, the prince orders him to return to the palace.

On his fourth and final excursion, Prince Siddhārtha encounters a mendicant. In some versions of the story, they do not speak to each other. The prince, impressed by the mendicant's serenity, asks his charioteer who he is, and learns that he is a man who has renounced the world. In a famous biography called *Deeds of the Buddha* (*Buddhacarita*), the prince speaks to the mendicant, who explains to the young man that he seeks to escape death and find a deathless state. After speaking these words, the mendicant flies into the sky.

The mendicant is an enigmatic figure in the story. After his enlightenment, the Buddha would often speak of four sufferings that afflict all humans: birth, aging, sickness, and death. According to the story, he had known none of them before venturing out in his chariot. His own birth had been blissful for both mother and child despite her death a week later, and he had been shielded from even the sight of the old, the sick, and the dead. The first three chariot rides present him with three types of suffering. The fourth suggests a remedy: as the Buddha, he would identify the nature of suffering and teach

others the path to escape it. The encounter with the mendicant lends a certain symmetry to the story, since the fourth
excursion from the four-walled palace offers the answer to the
question at the end of the prince's clockwise route. The mendicant also provides cultural context. In India at the time of the
Buddha there were many who had renounced the world—in
traditional terms, they were those who had left the household
and gone to dwell in the forest. Prince Siddhārtha would soon
become one of them.

Still, the presence of the mendicant might be pondered further. According to Buddhist doctrine, a Buddha appears in the
world only when the teachings of the previous Buddha have
been completely forgotten. At the time of Prince Siddhārtha's
birth, then, enlightenment was impossible because the path
to enlightenment was unknown. From this perspective, the
mendicant that the prince encounters may have sought a state
beyond death, but was doomed never to find it. The stories of
this encounter seem to acknowledge this dilemma. In one, the
charioteer is unable to answer the prince's question about the
mendicant's identity because prior to the Buddha's enlightenment, there are no mendicant monks. The gods have to provide
the answer to the charioteer, who then conveys it to the prince.
And in the *Deeds of the Buddha*, as noted earlier, the mendicant flies into the sky. The mendicant monk cannot show the
prince the true path because he would need to instruct him in
the teachings of the Buddha. However, the Buddha does not
yet exist since the prince is not yet enlightened.

The story of the prince's chariot rides raises a further
question. If the Buddha vowed billions of lifetimes earlier to

achieve Buddhahood and lead all beings to nirvana, and if as a bodhisattva he had been perfecting himself for eons in order to gain enlightenment, how could he have forgotten over a mere twenty-nine years that beings grow old, become sick, and die? Had he not declared at the moment of his birth that he had entered his last lifetime and would never be reborn again? It is said that the trauma of birth causes us to forget our former lives. But the prince suffered no trauma, emerging without pain from his mother's right side.

The accounts of the prince's youth seek to explain his amnesia. In one, meeting the old man causes him to remember sickness, old age, and death. In another, the four sights are all apparitions created by the gods, meant to spur the prince toward his renunciation of royal life and the salvation it will eventually bring to all beings, including the gods themselves. Indeed, in *Deeds of the Buddha*, the apparition of the corpse can be seen only by the prince and his charioteer, not by any others. That same text accounts for the presence of the mendicant monk when there were no Buddhist monks by explaining that the monk was in fact a god who was so long-lived that he had seen the Buddhas of the past and so took the form of a monk in order to inspire the prince.

According to still other accounts, the prince could not and did not forget his greater goal of enlightenment. Here and in accounts of later incidents in his life as the Buddha, we see the evidence of what might be called Buddhist docetism, borrowing the term from the early Christian heresy that claimed that God could not have suffered and died on the cross, that it had all been an illusion. In the Buddhist case, in texts like the *Vast Game* (*Lalitavistara*, a sūtra that likely dates from the third century CE) the chariot rides are all a performance. The prince never forgets who he is or what he seeks. Indeed, it is the prince himself who creates the old man, the sick man, the corpse, and the monk, and then asks his charioteer who they are, pretending not to know the answer. Were the life of the Buddha to lack the story of the four sights, as early versions seem to, and if the Buddha remembered all from the moment of his birth and proceeded in a straight line toward enlightenment, then there would be no dramatic tension in his story and there would be no turning point in his life. If the prince did not forget, then he could not remember. If there were no extremes, there could be no middle way, the famous teaching of the Buddha.

## The Women of the Inner Chambers

The *Great Matter* (*Mahāvastu*), the work regarded by scholars as the oldest biography of the Buddha, is believed to include elements dating from the second century BCE, although the text's present form dates from the fourth century CE. It contains two separate stories of the prince's renunciation; the second is the famous version that includes the chariot rides and Prince Siddhārtha's confrontation with his father. But in the first and likely earlier version, the Buddha describes his life as a prince in sixteen brief paragraphs, each beginning, "I was delicately, most delicately brought up, O monks." In the first of these paragraphs he goes on to say, "And while I was being thus delicately brought up, my Śākyan father caused to be built for me three palaces, for the cold, the warm and the rainy seasons, where I might divert, enjoy and amuse myself."[3] The tenth reads, "I was delicately, most delicately brought up, O monks. And while I was being thus delicately brought up, my Śākyan father provided me with the means of enjoying the five varieties of sensual pleasures, namely dance, song, music, orchestra and women, that I might divert, enjoy and amuse myself."[4] This is the only section of the text that mentions women; the other paragraphs describe the prince's sumptuous food, clothing, gardens, couches, garlands, and conveyances. After the extended description of his pleasures, the Buddha says:

> I was delicately, most delicately brought up, O monks. And while I was being thus delicately brought up, this thought occurred to me, "Now this life at home is too full of hindrances. The way of religious life is in the open air. It is not possible for one living at home to live the holy life that is utterly bright, blameless, pure and clean. Let me then, now go away from home into the homeless state."
>
> Then, O monks, against the wishes of my sobbing and weeping parents, I left my sumptuous home and universal kingship that was in my hands. And, now, being a wanderer from home into the homeless state, I withdrew towards the city of Vesālī and reached it.[5]

In this early version of the *Great Matter* there is no death of the prince's mother, no chariot rides, no confrontation between the prince and his father. Prince Siddhārtha is familiar with worldly pleasures, including the sensual pleasures of sexual desire, and sees them as hindrances to a holy life.

But in later versions of the life of the Buddha, the prince's father objects to his son's desire to renounce the world and sends beautiful women to employ the arts of love to prevent Prince Siddhārtha from renouncing the world. However, there is never any possibility that the future Buddha will succumb to temptation. In stories about his various dealings with these women, the prince's attitude is one of detached pity rather than of conflicted desire, unlike in the story of Prince Josaphat, as we shall see later. Part of Prince Siddhārtha's equanimity in the face of seductive beauty obviously derives from his exalted spiritual rank. The noble resolve of the prince is far stronger than the women's charms, and as the women of the palace entertain Prince Siddhārtha, he regards them impassively. Beautifully adorned, they play music, sing, and dance for the prince as instructed by the king, but Siddhārtha does not respond. Eventually the gods cause the women to collapse on the floor and fall asleep in unsightly postures: some drool, some grind their teeth, others snore or cough, while the prince remains seated on his golden throne.

The most famous Pali biography is the *Account of the Beginning* (*Nidānakathā*), dating from the fifth century CE. It describes the scene in this way: "He saw the disorder in which they were and became even more detached from sensual pleasures. The large terrace of his mansion, magnificently decorated and resembling the abode of Sakka [the king of the gods] appeared to him as a charnel ground full of corpses scattered here and there. The three states of existence seemed to him as a house in flames."[6] A longer description appears in the *Vast Game*. Here the prince surveys the sleeping women and in their beauty he sees only the body's inevitable degradation. He pronounces these verses:

> The body, born from the field of karma, issuing from the water of desire, is characterized by decay. Disfigured by tears and sweat, by saliva, urine, and blood, filled with filth from the belly, with marrow, blood, and liquids from the brain, always letting impurities flow—bodies are the abode of impure things and ugly stenches.

> Covered with leathery skin punctured by pores, teeth, and hair; weakened by the accumulation of excrement, pus, fat, and saliva; held together like a machine by sinews and nerves; made beautiful by the flesh but subject to the pains of disease; always tormented by hunger and thirst.

> This body with its many apertures is the abode of old age and death. Having seen this, what wise man would not look upon his own body as an enemy?[7]

The sight of the women causes the prince to reflect not on the loss of his own desire but on the impurity of the human body, full of vile fluids and filth. The body is an enemy not because it is subject to desire but because it is matter; it will grow old, die, and decay.

The most famous of these attempted seduction scenes occurs

in the *Deeds of the Buddha* by Aśvaghoṣa, a work usually dated
to the second century CE. In it, Prince Siddhārtha takes three
chariot rides. After seeing a corpse being carried down the
road, the prince orders his charioteer to return to the palace.
The charioteer, on prior instructions from the king, takes him
instead to a park, where beautiful women await him. Struck
by the facts of aging, sickness, and death, he rebuffs their
advances. When his friend asks him why he does not make
love to the women, the prince replies:

> I do not despise worldly objects, I know that all man-
> kind is bound up in them; but remembering that the
> world is transitory, my mind cannot find pleasure there.

> Old age, sickness, and death—if these three things did
> not exist, I too should find my enjoyment in the objects
> that please the mind. (IV.85–86)[8]

The prince shows no particular disdain for women or even for
the pleasures of the senses, acknowledging that others find
delight in them. But because life is marked by aging, sickness, and death, he is unable to find pleasure in bodily beauty
and desire.

He returns to the palace but soon goes out again, this time
on his steed Kaṇṭhaka. Coming to a field, he sees dead insects
and worms in the newly plowed furrows, farmers toiling in
the sun, and oxen straining at the yoke. Feeling compassion
for all of them, he sits down under a tree and practices meditation, achieving a state of concentration called the first *dhyāna*.

He then encounters the mendicant, who explains to the prince that he seeks release from birth and death and then flies into the sky. The prince returns to the palace and asks his father to grant him permission to renounce the world. Reflecting the traditional Indian view of the four stages of life (student, householder, forest dweller, and renunciant), the king explains that it is difficult for a young man to renounce the pleasures of the senses. It is not the time for the prince to renounce the throne. It is, instead, the appropriate time for the king himself to renounce the world and confer sovereignty upon his son. The prince agrees to remain in the world if his father will grant him four wishes: that he never die, that he never become sick, that he never grow old, and that he never lose his fortune. The king explains that these things are beyond his power: even the greatest sages fear old age, sickness, death, and misfortune. The prince then asks the king to allow him to leave, saying that it is not right to hold back a man who is trying to escape from a burning house. The prince leaves his father, and the king instructs his ministers to arrange the choicest pleasures to distract his son. Entering his inner chamber, the prince sits on a seat of gold and watches impassively as the women sing, dance, and play various musical instruments. As in other versions, the gods cause the women to fall asleep.

Aśvaghoṣa pauses over each of the sleeping women, describing their poses in erotic detail. Unlike other authors, he does not evoke the charnel ground. Yet the prince surveys the women with disgust:

Such is the nature of women, impure and monstrous in the world of living beings; but deceived by dress and ornaments a man becomes infatuated by a woman's attractions.

If a man would but consider the natural state of women and this change produced in them by sleep, assuredly he would not cherish his folly; but he is smitten by the thought of their elegance and so succumbs to passion. (V. 64–65)[9]

In sleep the artifice of beautiful garments and jewelry is stripped away, and the body that lies beneath is repugnant to the prince. And unlike the scene from the *Vast Game* described above, where the sight of the women causes the prince to reflect on the impurity of his own body and of the human body more generally, here what is revealed is the "true nature" of women, which should, in the prince's view, destroy the passion of any man who saw it clearly. Prince Siddhārtha's complete impassivity makes it clear that the women's charms are no match for his determination; his impassivity is a manifestation of an advanced spiritual state that allows him to perceive decay and death beneath the women's beautiful attire.

According to most accounts, the prince's son is born on the day that he renounces the world. Upon being informed that he is a father, the prince indicates his attitude toward family life, saying, "A fetter (*rāhu*) is born." And so the baby was named Rāhula. But in another version, found in both the *Great Matter* and in the monastic code of the Mūlasarvāstivādin order, after he decides to leave the world, the prince's last act before leaving the palace is to make love to his wife; Rāhula is not born that night but conceived.[10] Why would the future Buddha make love to his wife on the night of his departure from the palace? The text explains his motivation: "Lest others say that the Prince Śākyamuni was not a man, and that he wandered forth without paying attention to Yaśodharā, Gopikā, Mṛgajā, and his other sixty thousand wives, let me now make love to Yaśodharā."[11] After he makes loves to his wife, the prince falls asleep and has five dreams portending his enlightenment. In yet another version, he makes love to his wife to comfort her after she has had seven frightening dreams. In both versions, Rāhula is conceived that night. In *Barlaam and Josaphat*, we will see a different relationship between dreaming and the act of love.

Despite the Buddha's renunciation of women and sex, the standard descriptions of the Buddha's youth make sure to mention that he enjoyed the company of consorts and that he impregnated his wife. Buddhist literature pays particular attention to the Buddha's penis. The body of a Buddha is said to have the thirty-two marks of a superman (*mahāpuruṣa*), one of which is a penis hidden in a sheath, like that of a horse, but retractable inside his body so that it is invisible. The description of the Buddha's penis, like the account of his last night with his wife, suggests a complicated and sometimes contradictory attitude toward male sexuality in these texts. Only a man can become a monk, and according to the monastic code, he must answer a series of questions to confirm his gender before he could be ordained. Yet the Buddha's gender seems ambiguous: he is a virile male who fathered a son, but his penis retracts inside his body, making him appear genderless. The Buddha's lack of the attribute required for physical attachment is meaningful; it marks his spiritual detachment from the world.

In later Buddhist literature there is a small group of stories about the Buddha's hidden penis in which women, often prostitutes, spread rumors that the Buddha did not have a penis at all, leading in turn to its miraculous manifestation. In a fifth-century Chinese text, when the Buddha first reveals his male organ to a group of prostitutes, it appears as a flat and radiant disk. Rather than being impressed by this wondrous display, the women see it as confirmation of their claim that the Buddha lacks a functioning male member:

> When the Buddha heard this, [his organ] gradually emerged like that of a horse king. When it first appeared it was like the bodily organ of an eight-year-old boy, and it gradually grew into the shape of that of an adolescent. Seeing this, all the women rejoiced. Then the hidden organ gradually grew [and became] like a cylindrical banner of lotus flowers. In each layer there were ten billion lotuses; each lotus had ten billion jewel colors; each color had ten billion emanation Buddhas; and each emanation Buddha was served by one billion bodhisattvas and a boundless assembly.[12]

But such displays by the Buddha are rare, as are explicit calls for confirmations of the Buddha's virility.

In the *Great Matter* version of the Buddha's last night in the palace, a god comes to the prince and predicts what will happen in seven days:

> If, O Great Man, you will not leave home today, seven days hence the seven treasures of kingship will be pro-

duced and thou wilt become a universal king over the
four continents, triumphant, just, a king of justice, pos-
sessing the seven treasures. These seven treasures will
appear from the sky: the treasure of the wheel, of the
elephant, of the horse, of the jewel, of the woman, of the
householder, and of the counselor. And you will have a
full thousand sons who will be valiant, brave, comely,
overpowering the armies of their enemies, and noble.
You will hold and occupy in justice, without opposition,
without trouble, without recourse to violence and without oppression, these four great continents.[13]

The god's prediction is presented as a warning, and it is
a warning that the prince heeds—he leaves the palace that
night. But he does not leave immediately. Rather than father
one thousand sons, he fathers one. The next sentence after the
passage above is, "Rāhula . . . entered his mother's womb at
the hour of midnight." Prince Siddhārtha impregnates his wife
as his last worldly deed, a fulfillment of the duty that his father
demands.

## The Vow of Celibacy

Another story from after the Buddha's enlightenment may
suggest a different reason for the Buddha's final act of love with
his wife. In the time of the first days of the Buddha's community, the monks had no vows. The Buddha's first disciples all
gained enlightenment shortly after meeting him, and since the
conduct of an enlightened being is said to be inherently ethical,

rules to regulate their conduct were unnecessary. The need for rules arose only as the community of monks grew to include the unenlightened. Even then, the Buddha did not promulgate a comprehensive code of conduct. Instead, when a transgression occurred, the Buddha established a rule against it after the fact, without the original transgressor incurring punishment. There was thus a narrative of how each of the various rules in the monastic code came to be established. This is story of the rule requiring celibacy.

A young man named Sudinna, heir to a considerable fortune, was married but childless. After hearing the Buddha teach, he asked to join the order of monks. The Buddha told Sudinna that he needed the permission of his parents, who were aghast at the idea, relenting only when Sudinna refused food for six days. Sudinna was then ordained and immediately left his home village. A famine soon occurred, making it difficult for the monks to gather alms. Sudinna returned to his village where he hoped to find sufficient food for himself and his fellow monks. His parents, initially thinking that he was returning to the family, were disappointed to learn that he remained committed to the monastic life. His mother then went to him in his forest hermitage and explained that without an heir, their family line would come to an end and the parents' property would be seized by the king upon their death. Her request to her son, therefore, was not that he return to the family but that he produce an heir. Sudinna agreed. He met his wife in the forest when she was fertile, took off his monk's robes, and had intercourse with her three times. She conceived and bore a son who, according to the story, also became a monk. Sudinna never returned to his wife nor apparently felt any desire to do so.

Sudinna had broken no rule or vow, but he felt remorse for his deed and confessed it to his fellow monks. They in turn informed the Buddha, who famously declared, "Worthless man, it would be better that your penis be stuck into the mouth of a poisonous snake than into a woman's vagina. It would be better that your penis be stuck into the mouth of a black viper than into a woman's vagina. It would be better that your penis be stuck into a pit of burning embers, blazing and glowing, than into a woman's vagina. Why is that? For that reason you would undergo death or death-like suffering, but you would not on that account, at the break-up of the body, after death, fall into deprivation, the bad destination, the abyss, hell."[14]

The Buddha chastises Sudinna using a vividly misogynistic characterization of the female body as a warning to all monks of the dangers of physical intimacy with a woman. Sudinna was not expelled from the order. However, sexual intercourse (defined as the penetration of an orifice even to the depth of a sesame seed) would thereafter become one of four transgressions that entailed expulsion from the community of monks. The other three were killing a human, stealing, and lying about one's spiritual attainments.

This creation myth of the monastic rule of celibacy is not about love, or even passion, but obligation. Sudinna's beautiful wife does not seek him out because of desire, nor does Sudinna seek sexual pleasure with his wife. And it is not the case that love and lust are absent from the story because of some cultural reticence to represent them. Stories of love and longing abound in classical Indian literature. Sudinna responds to a request from his mother, not from his wife, and performs his filial (rather than spousal) duty. Yet the Buddha condemns the deed.

The story suggests that the Buddha censures not sex but what it leads to: birth and rebirth, the household they require, and the thoughts and emotions they produce. These are the engines of *saṃsāra*, the cycle of birth and death, the cycle from which the Buddha sought, and found, liberation. It is not that the Buddha somehow imagined that if the world were celibate, suffering would come to an end. Rather, the story suggests that he saw sex primarily as perpetuating *saṃsāra*, where so few could follow the path to nirvana. Sex also led to other problems. The entanglements created by sexual intercourse (which in this case means heterosexual intercourse) made progress to nirvana infinitely more difficult. As the prince says when he surveys the sleeping women who would seduce him, "Those whose judgment has been wrapped in the shadows of extreme confusion take the qualities of desire for virtues; like birds that enter traps, they lose their freedom."[15] The goal of the Buddhist path is not creation but extinction, like a flame going out. Even the Buddha's family line will come to an end when Rāhula, the sole son of the Buddha, also becomes a celibate monk.

## The Bodhisattva Becomes the Buddha

The prince leaves the palace in the middle of the night, pausing to gaze at his sleeping wife and infant son. He wants to hold his son one last time, but does not do so, fearing that it will awaken his wife and that he will lose his resolve to renounce the world. He promises to return after he has found the deathless state.

Despite the poignancy of this moment, the prince's departure from the palace is represented as a momentous and epochal event, and the gods rejoice that the prince has now resumed the quest for Buddhahood that he began so many lifetimes ago. Miracles and auspicious portents attend his departure. The king had instructed his troops to lock the gates of the palace and patrol the walls. But the guards fall asleep and the prince, mounted on his loyal steed with his charioteer holding onto the horse's tail, easily leaps over the walls of the palace. Once outside, he wishes to take one last look at the palace and the world he is about to leave behind. Knowing his wish, the deity of the earth pivots the spot where the steed stands so that the prince can gaze at the city without turning back. As he then proceeds on his horse into the forest, his way lit by torches held aloft by gods, the horse's progress is impeded by great piles of flowers that fall from the sky.

Once he reaches the forest, the prince becomes a monk, exchanging his royal raiment for the simple robes of his charioteer. He cuts off his long locks with his sword and throws his topknot into the air, saying that if he is to achieve Buddhahood, may the topknot not descend. The topknot is caught by a god, who enshrines it in heaven. From that point, the Buddha never cuts his hair or shaves his face, and his hair remains in the curls so familiar from Buddhist art. He dismisses his charioteer, telling him to inform his parents that he is well. He also bids farewell to his horse, who immediately dies of a broken heart. The prince, now alone, proceeds to another city, where he begs for alms, overcoming his nausea at the taste of food so different from the delicacies of the palace. He is noticed by the local king, who is so impressed by the monk's demeanor that he goes to speak with him. According to one account, the king offers the prince command of an army; according to another, he offers him his throne, yet another example of the parallel between kingship and Buddhahood in his story. The prince refuses all the offers and promises to return after achieving his goal. His first attempts to find the deathless state lead him, in succession, to two different meditation teachers. In each case, the prince quickly masters their methods and equals their attainments, concluding that they offer sublime states of concentration, but are not paths to liberation from birth and death.

Next, he undertakes a rigorous regimen of self-mortification in the company of five other ascetics, known to tradition simply as "the group of five." Sometimes he goes naked, sometimes dressed in tree bark, sometimes dressed in a cloak made from human hair, sometimes dressed in burial shrouds. He sleeps on beds of nails and on the bones of the dead. Sometimes he bathes three times a day; sometimes he goes so long without bathing that his body is caked with dirt. He lives outdoors in all seasons, both day and night. He eats fallen fruit and grass and cow dung, and sometimes his own excrement. Children spit at him and urinate on him. Sometimes he eats only once each fortnight. At the end of the six years of such practices, he has fasted to the brink of starvation, consuming only one grain of rice and one sesame seed a day until his buttocks are like a bull's hoof, his backbone protrudes like a cord of beads, and his eyes sink into their sockets. In Lahore, there is a famous statue of the skeletal prince seated in the meditation posture. He eventually faints from malnutrition, and when he regains consciousness, he concludes that six years of ascetic practices have not led him closer to his goal. He thus begs for alms in a nearby village, regaining his strength but earning the scorn of his five companions, who abandon him. Having now learned that enlightenment is not to be found in either extreme—the indulgence of the body that he knew as a prince or the mortification of the body that he has known as an ascetic—he sets out alone.

On the fateful day of his enlightenment, he accepts a meal of milk rice from a maiden who mistakes him for a tree spirit. He then accepts some handfuls of grass (to be used as a seat) from a grass cutter. Identifying the sacred Bodhi tree, he stands on the south side of the tree facing north, but the world tilts wildly, dipping to the south. This happens two more times, until the prince stands on the eastern side of the tree, facing west. When the earth does not move, he scatters a bundle of grass on the ground and sits down under the tree, facing east. One final trial lies ahead.

In Buddhism, Māra is the deity of desire and death. On the day that the prince would achieve enlightenment, Māra fears that Siddhārtha is about to pass beyond his dominion by escaping the grip of desire and death, and he sends hosts of demons against the prince in a battle between the powers of worldly darkness and the powers of spiritual light. The demons, led by Māra's sons—Confusion, Arousal, and Pride—are armed with frightful weapons to attack the prince, who is seated alone beneath the tree armed only with the ten perfections, which he has practiced over millions of past lifetimes. Māra causes a great whirlwind, but the hem of the prince's robe does not stir. Māra causes a torrential rain, but the prince's robe remains dry. A hail of weapons launched by Māra's minions turns into bouquets of flowers, hot ashes turn into sandalwood powder, and a rain of mud turns into a soothing ointment. Finally, Māra casts his huge razor-edged discus at the prince, but it stops in midair above the prince's head and turns into a canopy of garlands.

In some accounts, when he cannot unseat the prince, Māra sends his three daughters, Lust, Craving, and Discontent, to seduce the Buddha. Knowing the range of objects of male desire, they each transform themselves into one hundred different beautiful women for the prince to choose among, each skilled in the thirty-two arts of seduction. Yet the prince remains unmoved. Next, they seek to determine the age of the woman who would attract the Buddha. First each of the daughters is one hundred girls, then one hundred young women who have not yet given birth, then one hundred women who have given birth once, then one hundred women who have given birth twice, then one hundred middle-aged women, then one hundred old women (in some texts, in order to arouse his pity; in others, to arouse his lust). The Buddha remains unmoved in each case, but he is not impassive. He uses his magical powers to lock the daughters of Māra into the last of their transformations. "Bending their feet, with decrepit limbs, they addressed their father: 'O father . . . the lord of the world of Desire, restore us to our own forms.'" But such a restoration is beyond Māra's powers. The women then seek refuge in the Buddha, who restores them to their youthful forms.

Finally, Mara challenges the prince's right to occupy the

small parcel of earth beneath the tree, asking him what gift he has given to do so. Having no witness to testify to the myriad acts of generosity that he has performed over his many past lives, the prince touches the earth with his right hand, calling on the goddess of the earth to bear witness. She does so with a tremor. It is this posture, rather than one in which his hands are joined in his lap in the posture of meditation, in which the Buddha is most commonly depicted in painting and sculpture across the Buddhist world. The posture of "touching the earth" suggests the Buddha's dominion over the world.

Having defeated Māra and his minions, the prince now begins to meditate. In ancient India, the night was divided into the three periods of a guard's duty. In the first watch of the night, the prince has a vision of all of his past lives. In the second watch, he understands how beings rise and fall according to their deeds; that is, he understands the workings of the law of karma. In the third watch, he destroys all the causes for his future rebirth. The exact content of this third and most consequential period of meditation is the subject of much commentary in Buddhist literature, but all agree that he understood how ignorance leads to suffering and rebirth, and that he understood it so fully that he would never be reborn again. At dawn, he was the Buddha, a Sanskrit term most commonly translated as "awakened." His enlightenment occurred on his thirty-fifth birthday.

It is said that the Buddha remained in the vicinity of the Bodhi tree for the next seven weeks, eating nothing and sustained only by the power of his attainment. Seven weeks, or forty-nine days, would later be codified as the maximum amount of time in the "intermediate state" between death in one lifetime and rebirth in the next. At the end of that period, the Buddha accepts his first meal from two passing merchants and gives them some of his hair. Significantly, the first thing that the new Buddha offers to the world is not instructions to be practiced on the path to enlightenment but rather relics to be venerated.

Many miraculous events occur during these days. Although the Buddha had been striving toward this enlightenment for eons, he is here represented as unsure of what to do next, as feeling that what he has understood is too profound to be understood by others. In an important scene, the god Brahmā descends from his heaven to implore the Buddha to teach. In Buddhism, gods have vast powers, sublime pleasures, and long lifespans, but they are also bound in the cycle of birth, death, and rebirth. The Buddha, although a human, has a knowledge that the gods do not have. Brahmā explains that although some beings are too benighted to benefit from his teachings, some have "little dust in their eyes." The Buddha complies, agreeing to teach. The question is to whom. He feels that his two former meditation teachers would be the most worthy and appropriate, but they have recently died. He then decides to teach the group of five who left him when he abandoned the regimen of strict asceticism.

After walking a distance of many miles, the Buddha finds the group of five in a park outside the great city of Banaras. Referring to himself as "the Tathāgata," that is, "the one who has thus gone," he delivers what is sometimes called his first sermon, which begins, "Monks, these two extremes should not be followed by one who has gone forth into homelessness. What two? The pursuit of sensual happiness in sensual pleasures, which is low, vulgar, the way of worldlings, ignoble, unbeneficial; and the pursuit of self-mortification, which is painful, ignoble, unbeneficial. Without veering towards either of these extremes, the Tathāgata has awakened to the middle way, which gives rise to vision, which gives rise to knowledge, which leads to peace, to direct knowledge, to enlightenment, to nirvana."[16] This is his first articulation of the "middle way" of Buddhism, in this case, the middle way between the extreme of self-indulgence, which he had known as a prince in the palace, and the extreme of self-mortification, which he had known as an ascetic in the wilderness. In the same sermon, the Buddha goes on to delineate the four noble truths: that life is qualified by suffering; that that suffering has a cause; that there exists a state of the cessation of suffering called nirvana; and that there is a path to that state of cessation. Shortly after hearing the sermon, each of the five also achieves liberation from rebirth. Still, their enlightenment is different from that of the Buddha, in part because he was able to find the path to nirvana without a teacher.

Biographies of the Buddha tend to devote most of their attention to the events described so far. The Buddha is said to have lived for eighty years, but the period between his enlightenment and his death is generally passed over rather quickly, with emphasis reserved for the momentous events surrounding his passage into nirvana. However, narratives about the Buddha's life after his enlightenment do recount the conversion of particular disciples, both those who become monks and those kings and merchants who become the Buddha's patrons. Conversions occur individually and en masse. The tradition in ancient India was that if the teacher converted, all of his disciples also must convert. In a memorable scene, the Buddha's success in converting a large group of Hindu ascetics is inferred by others when they see long locks floating down the river. Long-haired Hindus had become bald Buddhist monks. A particularly significant group conversion takes place when the Buddha establishes (grudgingly, according to the story) an order of nuns, at the request of his stepmother and the wives and mothers of men ordained when he returned to his home city after his enlightenment.

## The Buddha Returns Home

This return, when the Buddha meets his father and his wife again, is an important event. After hearing of his son's enlightenment, the king sends a series of envoys to invite him back to the capital, but in each case the envoy hears the Buddha's teaching, joins the order of monks, and forgets to convey the invitation. It is only after ten envoys have been sent that the message is finally delivered. When the Buddha enters his father's city, his elders are reluctant to pay homage to a younger man of their clan until the Buddha levitates, at which point they bow before him. When the king looks out the window of the palace and sees his son going from door to door begging for alms, he is aghast and chides him: such behavior is beneath the dignity of his royal lineage. The Buddha replies that his lineage is not that of kings but of Buddhas, and Buddhas beg for alms. The king relents and receives his son's teachings, achieving the first of the four levels of enlightenment.

The Buddha's wife, still stung by his desertion and the gossip she subsequently suffered, refuses to go to see him, demanding that he come to her, which he eventually does. In some versions of their encounter, she berates him for leaving her alone with an infant child, but eventually also becomes his disciple and later a nun. At one point, she sends the Buddha's young son, Rāhula, to his father to request his patrimony, assuming that as the grandson of the king, Rāhula will be made crown prince. Again playing on the tension between kingship and Buddhahood, the Buddha ordains his son instead of designating him as his royal heir, to the great dismay of the Buddha's father. In response to a request from his father, the Buddha promises that in the future any children who seek ordination must have the permission of their parents. The Buddha then leaves the city, followed by a number of his kinsmen who have decided to become monks. When the Buddha later learns that his father is near death, he uses his magical powers to fly back to the city, where he teaches his father once again. The king passes through the three other stages of enlightenment and enters nirvana at death.

Among the kinsmen who departed with the Buddha was the Buddha's half-brother, the handsome Nanda. On the third day of the Buddha's visit to Kapilavastu, Nanda is to be married. The Buddha enters his house and offers good wishes, but then hands Nanda his begging bowl and abruptly leaves; this is a famous scene in Buddhist iconography, with the Buddha departing on one side, Nanda's beautiful bride-to-be on the other, and Nanda standing in the middle, holding the bowl, wondering which way he should turn. As his betrothed beckons to him, Nanda follows the Buddha into a grove, where the Buddha convinces him to become a monk. Nanda, however, remains consumed with thoughts of his beautiful bride-to-be after his ordination, and finally goes to the Buddha to tell him that he has decided to return to lay life and his wife. The Buddha then takes him on a magical journey to the Heaven of the Thirty-three. On the way, the Buddha points out a red-faced, one-eyed female monkey—in some versions, she is described more graphically as a monkey whose ears, nose, and tail have been cut off—sitting on a charred tree stump. The Buddha asks Nanda which is more beautiful, the monkey or his fiancée, and Nanda replies somewhat indignantly that there is no comparison between the two.

When they arrive in the heaven, Nanda sees the beautiful celestial nymphs who attend the gods, "enrapturing the weary minds of ascetics who had decided to buy heaven by first paying the price in ascetic practices. . . . Eternally youthful and occupied solely with lovemaking, they were a communal enjoyment for heaven-dwellers who had earned merit. Taking heavenly women as lovers was no fault, just an acceptance of the rewards of asceticism."[17] To Nanda, the human world looks like a charnel ground when compared to heaven, and he is overcome with lust for the nymphs. This is not a weakness on Nanda's part. According to the story, any human male who saw the nymphs would have been driven mad; it is only the protection of the Buddha that saves Nanda.

The Buddha asks Nanda whether he prefers the celestial

nymphs or his human bride. Nanda replies that compared to the nymphs, she looks like the ugly monkey. The Buddha then explains that through the practice of purity (the term is *brahma-carya* in Sanskrit, and often means "celibacy") on earth, he will be reborn in the Heaven of the Thirty-three among these nymphs. This promise cures Nanda of his lustful thoughts for his earthly bride. However, when he returns to the city, he mentions the heavenly reward that awaits him to other monks, and they mock him for his motivation. Their jibes cause him to turn his thoughts away from heaven and toward nirvana, and he soon attains enlightenment.

This is the story as it appears in a poem by Aśvaghoṣa, the same poet who wrote the *Deeds of the Buddha*. In another version, Nanda's renunciation is motivated not by a vision of heaven but by the horrors of hell. When the Buddha takes Nanda to heaven, they find one palace filled with beautiful nymphs but no gods. When Nanda asks the nymphs why there are no gods present, they reply that they are waiting for the arrival of a monk named Nanda who, because he renounced the world, will be reborn as a god there after he dies. Then the Buddha takes Nanda to hell, where they see demons stoking fires under cauldrons filled with the damned. One of the cauldrons is empty. When Nanda asks the demon fueling the fire why it is empty, the demon replies that it is reserved for a monk named Nanda who, because he returned to lay life, will be reborn in the cauldron after he dies. Nanda becomes enlightened seven days later.[18]

The Buddha's celestial journey with Nanda was not his only visit to heaven. When he returned to his home city, he could not visit his mother because she had died seven days after his birth and was reborn in the Joyous Heaven, the same heaven from which the bodhisattva had chosen his birthplace and parents for his final lifetime. His mother, therefore, had not lived long enough to benefit from her son's teachings. In order to remedy this lack, in the seventh year after his enlightenment, the Buddha uses his magical powers to ascend to the Heaven of the Thirty-three atop Mount Meru—the central mountain in the Buddhist cosmos—where his mother, now a male deity, descends from the Joyous Heaven to meet him. He spends the three months of the summer rainy season (during which monks stay in retreat) teaching the *dharma* to the assembled gods, returning to earth briefly each day to collect alms and pausing to give a disciple a summary of what he has been teaching the gods. One of the Buddha's patrons, King Udayana, is devastated when he learns that he will be unable to behold the Buddha for three months and so asks a monk with magical powers to transport a five-foot piece of sandalwood and thirty-two artists to the Heaven of the Thirty-three, where together they are to carve a statue of the Buddha. Each artist is responsible for depicting one of the thirty-two marks of a superman that adorn the Buddha's body. When the sandalwood statue is complete, it returns to earth with the artists. When the Buddha eventually makes his triumphal descent from heaven, the statue rises to meet him, and it is thereafter a standing image of the Buddha. According to one tradition, it is this very image that Chinese envoys bring from India and present to the emperor when Buddhism first comes to China.

## The Death of the Buddha

In his final year, the Buddha is again approached by Māra, who reminds him of the promise he had extracted from him at the time of enlightenment: to pass into nirvana when his work was done. The Buddha concedes that he has done what he had set out to do. However, he intimates to his personal attendant and cousin, the monk Ānanda, that before passing away into nirvana a Buddha can live "for an eon or until the end of an eon" if he is asked to do so. The Buddha mentions the possibility three times, but Ānanda fails to take the hint, and so the Buddha decides to pass away. After accepting a meal of "pig's delight" (generally thought to be pork; contrary to popular belief, the Buddha was not a vegetarian), the Buddha becomes ill and asks Ānanda to prepare a bed for him on the ground between two trees, with the head of the bed pointing north. As the Buddha lies down on his right side between the two trees, they immediately bloom.

The scene of the Buddha's death is one of the most famous in Buddhist art. He is surrounded by weeping monks, nuns, deities, and laypeople. In one genre of Japanese painting even the animals of the forest are crying, with elephants, lions, and rabbits wracked with sobs. The Buddha then bestows his final instructions to the order of monks. Ānanda asks how to pay respect to the Buddha after he has passed away. The Buddha declares that people should visit four places: the sites of his birth, enlightenment, and first teaching, and this, the site of his nirvana. Anyone who dies while on pilgrimage to one of these four places will be reborn as a god in heaven. The Buddha does not appoint a successor, saying that after he is gone, the *dharma* and the *vinaya*, the doctrine and the discipline, will teach the people. Finally, the Buddha reminds his monks that everything eventually passes away. He then goes into a state of deep meditation, proceeding through various stages, before passing into nirvana.

The Buddha's final words also include instructions for his funeral. At the time of his death, the Buddha instructs Ānanda to give him the funeral of a *cakravartin*, a wheel-turning monarch. The body is to be wrapped in a thousand alternating layers of new cotton cloth and carded cotton cloth and then placed in an iron casket filled with oil. The funeral pyre of perfumed woods should then be lit. After the fire has gone out, the relics should be collected and enshrined in a dome-shaped structure called a *stūpa*, which was to be erected at a crossroads.

But the pyre does not light; one of the Buddha's closest disciples is not present. When he eventually arrives, the pyre spontaneously bursts into flame. Groups of the Buddha's lay disciples soon arrive, and a battle ensues over who should receive the relics. Eventually, the relics are divided into eight portions. These eight, plus the remaining pile of ashes and the bucket used to divide the relics, are distributed to the competing groups, and ten *stūpas* are erected. Some two centuries later, the great emperor Aśoka broke open these *stūpas* and redistributed the relics, making, it is said, eighty-four thousand *stūpas*. In the nineteenth century, as officers of the British Raj built roads and railways across the Indian subcontinent, they unearthed some of these *stūpas* and opened the stone caskets to reveal what are said to be relics of the Buddha.

Not long after his enlightenment, the Buddha had said to his monks, "Go forth, O monks, and wander, for the welfare of the many, for the happiness of the many, out of compassion for the world, for the benefit, welfare, and happiness of gods and humans. Let no two take the same road." In the centuries after his death, the teachings of the Buddha spread far beyond the area of northeastern India where he had taught. The emperor Aśoka ruled an empire that encompassed much of modern India and Pakistan. He was a patron of Buddhism and erected commemorative pillars at important sites connected to the life of the Buddha. According to Buddhist sources, he was very devout, dispatching Buddhist missionaries to foreign lands, including his own son (a monk) and his daughter (a nun), who brought Buddhism to the island of Sri Lanka. In the second century CE, the emperor Kaniṣka of the Kushan Dynasty was also a great patron of Buddhism. His capital was in Peshawar in what is today northwest Pakistan and his rule extended far into modern Afghanistan.

From this region, Buddhist monks would take Buddhism to China in the first century CE; it spread to Korea in the fourth century and from Korea to Japan in the sixth century. Buddhism spread to Tibet in the seventh century, and it also spread south to Thailand, Burma, Cambodia, Laos, and Vietnam. One of the greatest Buddhist monuments in the world, Borobudur, on the island of Java, was built in the ninth century.

We associate Buddhism with India, Sri Lanka, China, Korea, Tibet, and the countries of Southeast Asia because Buddhism remains a presence there. We tend to forget how important Buddhism was in what are today Pakistan, Afghanistan, and

Iran, in regions once known by names like Scythia, Bactria, Parthia, and Sogdiana. The earliest Buddhist manuscripts, some dating from the first century BCE, were discovered in a cave in Afghanistan. In the sixth century, the massive Buddhas of Bamiyan were carved out of sandstone cliffs. Chinese Buddhist monks who passed through Afghanistan on pilgrimage to the holy places of India as late as the seventh century report a vibrant Buddhist community there, with many monks, monasteries, and shrines containing relics of the Buddha.

Buddhism was also a major presence in Persia, surviving a persecution by the Sassanids in 224 CE, and remained a major presence until the coming of Islam in the seventh century. At the time of the Muslim conquest, which was completed in 651 CE, the story of the Buddha was known in Persia and may have been written down in Persian, although no versions survive. The story of the Buddha does survive, however, in Arabic, the sacred language of the Muslims.

# CHAPTER TWO

# The Buddha Becomes a Prophet:
# The Arabic *Bilawhar and Būdhāsaf*

The story of the Buddha's life traveled out of India, probably following one of the ancient trading routes connecting
China, India, Persia, and Syria, known collectively as the Silk
Road. Traders and travelers transported silk across deserts
and mountains along these routes, along with minerals, spices,
metals, saddles, leather goods, glass, and paper. They also carried stories.[1] Literary and religious narratives traveled west-
ward in both oral and written form, and many were translated
into Pahlavi, or Middle Persian, when they reached the Sassa-
nian empire in what is present-day Iran. Scholars assume that
Buddhist texts followed this path, and although the Pahlavi
translation of the Buddha's story has been lost, it is likely to
have been the basis for the Arabic *Bilawhar and Būdhāsaf*,
which preserves several episodes from the life of the Buddha
even as it elaborates the prince's relationship to his father and
adds a teacher who comes to instruct the prince on the values
of the ascetic renunciation of the world.

We know that the Arabic *Kitāb Bilawhar wa Būdhāsaf* ("The Book of Bilawhar and Būdhāsaf") was composed before the end of the tenth century CE because it is listed in a catalog of Arabic books available in Baghdad bookshops at that time. The catalog also identifies a reworking of the story in verse by an author known to have died in or around 815 CE, so if the reference is accurate, an early version of *Bilawhar and Būdhāsaf* would have been composed before the late eighth century CE, during the rule of the Abbasids, the third Islamic caliphate.[2] Shortly after the Abbasids gained power in a revolt against the Umayyad caliphate in 750 CE, the center of the Islamic empire moved from Damascus, the Umayyad's capital, to Baghdad, a city built by the Abbasids after the Muslim conquest of the Persian Sasanian empire. As an Arab-Persian Abbasid elite succeeded the Arab Umayyad elite, a new openness to ethnic and cultural difference appeared among scholars, manifested in greater inclusion of non-Arab Muslims in the administration of the empire and an interest in non-Arab cultures and philosophy. Translations began to bring texts and traditions from outside the Arab world to Muslim scholars, and this interest in non-Arab cultures and texts may explain the interest of *Bilawhar and Būdhāsaf* to Islamic audiences.[3]

Two versions of *Bilawhar and Būdhāsaf* survive. Both draw on an unidentified Buddhist account of the life of the Buddha, translated from Sanskrit or another Indian language into Pahlavi, and both add stories and sermons taken from Arabic literary sources. We know that some of the stories are taken from a Pahlavi collection of maxims and exemplary stories composed in the sixth century. Like other Pahlavi texts, the collection was probably translated into Arabic by Muslims of

Persian descent and then incorporated into a story based on the life of the Buddha, supplemented with exemplary stories and parables drawn from other Arabic sources and illustrating, for the most part, the lessons of a teacher who comes to instruct the prince.[4]

Both extant versions of *Bilawhar and Būdhāsaf* are associated with sects of Shi'a Islam. During the centuries following the death of the Prophet Muhammad, the Shi'ite Muslims split into different factions, mainly due to disputes over succession to the office of imam. The longer of the two versions of *Bilawhar and Būdhāsaf* is associated with the Ismaili branch of Shi'a Islam and is preserved in manuscripts in Yemen and western India, where the sect was strong. It does not reflect specifically Ismaili doctrine, but was probably considered a work on ethics and asceticism that was more generally compatible with Islamic belief.[5] Abridged versions of the book are found outside the Ismaili collections, further evidence that it circulated as a work that appealed to Muslim readers, although not regarded as a book specifically about Islam.

A second, shorter version of *Bilawhar and Būdhāsaf* is cited in a treatise by the influential Twelver Shi'ite author Ibn Bābūya (d. 991 CE). It may be based on the longer version, or on a lost earlier redaction of the story. A large part of the middle section of the story is missing in this version, either because of a lacuna in the source or because Ibn Bābūya did not wish to include it, and a series of seven stories taken from existing literary sources has been added to fill the gap.[6] Ibn Bābūya explains that he uses the Bilawhar story to draw readers to the rest of his treatise, which promotes the beliefs of his sect.

"Whether readers agree or disagree with us, they all enjoy such stories, and if they find some in this book, they will want to read the rest of it," he writes. For Ibn Bābūya the story of the prince who renounces the world will attract readers, who will then read the doctrinal discussions included in his book and learn the true path to belief.[7]

Although *Bilawhar and Būdhāsaf* found a readership among Muslims, it does not mention the Prophet Muhammad and there is only one brief reference to Islam. Nor does the story clearly identify Buddhism, as we will see below. The narrator calls the ascetic religion adopted by the king's son, Būdhāsaf, and persecuted by his father simply "the Religion" (we will capitalize in this usage). We learn, for example, that the king, here named Junaysar, "persecuted followers of the Religion and banned them from his lands in order to surround himself with idolaters."[8] *Dīn*, the Arabic word used for "the Religion," has a wide range of meaning. It originally denoted obedience or discipline and later came to signify obedience to the precepts of Islam. It can also refer to customs or habits, and is even used to indicate debt or financial obligation. With the valorization of *dīn*, the Arabic text does not overtly promote Islam; in fact, the only explicit mention of Islam in the text is in the conclusion, where Būdhāsaf, at his death, claims to have "assembled the flock of Islam that had been dispersed." Nor does "the Religion" suggest a veiled form of Buddhism. Although *Bilawhar and Būdhāsaf* borrows its frame from the life of the Buddha, the religious doctrine it describes is foreign to Buddhism. In fact, as the editor of the anonymous longer version of *Bilawhar and Būdhāsaf* notes, the large place given to the persecution of the "people of the Religion" by idolaters, the exaltation of martyrs, and the monotheism of Būdhāsaf's teacher Bilawhar are closer to a Syrian Christian tradition than to Indian Buddhism.[9]

Both Arabic versions begin with the birth of Būdhāsaf, and their description of the prince's early life and later death are similar to the Buddhist accounts. Apart from that resemblance, there are no other examples of early Arabic narratives about the life of the Buddha. In fact, early Muslim historians appear to have had little knowledge about Buddhism. Al-Bīrūnī's early eleventh-century encyclopedia on India, *Verifying All That the Indians Recount, the Reasonable and the Unreasonable*, gives many details about Hinduism, but relatively few descriptions of Buddhism.[10]

However, the lack of accurate information about Buddhist practices and beliefs does not mean that early Muslim writers had no knowledge of Buddhism's founder.[11] The Buddha's name was preserved in two forms in Arabic texts: *al-Budd*, derived from *Buddha*, and *Būdhāsaf*, derived from *bodhisattva*. The two forms almost always appear separately; the first is used as a common noun to name an idol or as a proper name to represent a divinity or a prophet.[12] Only rarely is *al-Budd* associated with the Buddha, as in this exceptional account of Buddhist belief by the Muslim writer al-Shahrastānī in the early twelfth century:

> The Buddha [*al-Budd*], in their opinion, means a person who is not born, who never marries nor eats food nor drinks nor grows old nor dies. The first Buddha appearing in the world was named *Shākamīn*, which

means 'the noble master'. Five thousand years have elapsed from the time of his appearance and the time of the *hijra* [622 CE]. They assert that below the rank of the Buddha is the rank of the Būdīsaʿīya [Bodhisattva], the latter term meaning, "the one who seeks the way of the truth." Indeed, one arrives at this rank only by: patience and alms-giving; seeking after that which ought to be sought; abstinence and withdrawal from the world, and aloofness from its desires and pleasures; abstinence from what is forbidden; compassion for all created beings; avoidance of the ten offenses.[13]

This description demonstrates knowledge of the Buddha's relation to a bodhisattva and uses *al-Budd* as the name of the Buddha, but again, this is an exceptional account and the connection of *al-Budd* to the historical Buddha remains rare in Muslim accounts.

In the passage above, as in Buddhism, the Sanskrit word *bodhisattva*, from which *Būdhāsaf* is derived, is the term for someone who aspires to become a Buddha. It is also the term that the Buddha used when describing himself in the time before his enlightenment, including his past lives, as we noted in Chapter One. However, early Muslim texts do not clearly distinguish between a bodhisattva and a Buddha, nor do they demonstrate a clear understanding of who the Buddha was. Many Muslim historians take Būdhāsaf to be a semi-mythical character from early human times; some claim that he existed before Adam. In the Persian poet Firdawsī's *Book of the Kings*, written at the end of the tenth century, he is a false prophet who appeared in India at the time of Tamūrhaṭ, the third king of the world. This Būdhāsaf taught the so-called Sabaean religion, which some historians take to be the Chaldean belief in the divinity of the elements. The tenth-century Arabic historian al-Masʻūdī says this about Būdhāsaf's teaching:

> A star's departure from its sphere, its course through space, the converging or separation of stars at a single point determine, according to Būdhāsaf, everything that happens in the world, the duration of life, the composition of simple compounds and the dissolution of composed matter, the shape of exterior forms, the appearance or absorption of water into the earth. In sum, he located the supreme engine of the universe in the planets and their spheres.[14]

In this passage, Būdhāsaf is said to teach that the stars move the universe and shape everything that happens in it; he is a teacher or a sage. According to other Muslim historians, Būdhāsaf was a false prophet; others saw him as the founder of an idolatrous religion in India. It appears that Būdhāsaf was also remembered for preaching asceticism and generosity, but the more famous teachings of the Buddha, including the four noble truths, do not appear in Muslim texts, nor do these texts recount the Buddha's life.[15] Only *Bilawhar and Būdhāsaf* includes a version of the Buddha's life story.

Historian Daniel Gimaret has suggested that in the Islamic tradition, it is as though Buddhism was shattered into fragments that no one knew how to reassemble.[16] Such fragmentary knowledge is not surprising. As Islam began to spread in the seventh century CE, Buddhism was disappearing in India, especially in its northwestern area (modern Afghanistan and Pakistan) where the earliest Muslim contact had occurred. The famous Chinese pilgrim Xuanzang, traveling through the region in the first half of the seventh century, reported that many Buddhist monasteries were in ruins. Moreover, whereas early Muslim scholars assimilated many scientific texts from India, translations of Indian philosophical texts were much less common. *Bilawhar and Būdhāsaf* is the rare text that reproduces the story of the Buddha's life, though here it serves as a frame for a series of exemplary stories and parables that promote ascetic values. Its Muslim audiences most likely saw the narrative as a text by a non-Muslim writer which nonetheless illustrated values compatible with Islam.

## A Prince Is Born

*Bilawhar and Būdhāsaf* opens with the story of a king who desires a son, and all subsequent translations and rewritings of the story preserve this narrative frame.[17] In the Arabic version, this king is Junaysar of India, and he rules Sūlābaṭ, a place name that may be a deformation of Kapilavastu (or in Pali, Kapilavatthu), the birthplace of the Buddha. Junaysar is an idolater king, much attached to the pleasures and glories of his position, and he persecutes the "people of the Religion"; as we said earlier, "the Religion" names an ascetic renunciation of worldly values. But one of the king's courtiers adopts these ascetic beliefs. King Junaysar learns of it and confronts him, demanding that he explain his conversion. The courtier delivers a long sermon on the vanities of the world, the fleeting nature of its pleasures, and the need to prepare for a future life, thus offering the king and the story's readers an initial primer on ascetic beliefs. The king reviles his courtier's path, exiles him, and continues to persecute all those who turn away from the worship of idols.

In King Junaysar we have a very different ruler from Prince Siddhārtha's father. King Śuddhodana is a just and respected king. He is not a zealot and he does not persecute his subjects. In one sense, he may be termed an idolater because he makes offerings to various gods, but this religion of ancient India is not a practice that his son, even after he becomes the Buddha, specifically condemns.

In the Arabic story, King Junaysar longs for a son to continue his lineage, and his wife has a dream that foretells the birth of a son called Būdhāsaf. In its inclusion of the mother's prophetic dream, *Bilawhar and Būdhāsaf* preserves an element of the Buddhist narrative absent from Ibn Bābūya's Arabic version and from later Christian versions of the story. All versions of the story agree, however, that the king summons astrologers to foretell his son's future. They similarly foretell that the king's son will attain honors and privileges, but one astrologer who reveals that the prince will be a leader of the ascetics and that his glory will come in the next world. Again, the king builds a palace for the prince, isolates him from all the ills of the world, and surrounds him with beauty and pleasure. However, King Junaysar, unlike King Śuddhodana, fears the prophecy and intensifies his persecution of the people of the Religion.

The Arabic story moves away from the Indian work at this point. In the Arabic version, the king has a favored minister who is devoted to his sovereign and serves him faithfully. The minister has great power in the court and the king's other courtiers are jealous of his friend. One day the minister is out hunting and comes upon a man who has been gravely wounded by a wild animal. The man asks for his help and promises a great reward to the minister in exchange for his succor. The minister asks what reward he would receive and the wounded man replies that he mends words with words; when he finds a tear, he repairs it, restitching it so that no ill results. The minister pays little attention to the man's claim, but takes him home and cares for him.

Meanwhile, the king's courtiers conspire to destroy the favored minister. They tell Junaysar that he plans to claim the throne after the king's death. They counsel the king to test his minister's loyalty by summoning him and telling the man that he has decided to abandon his rule and join the ascetics. The minister's reaction will allow the king to judge his intentions, they claim.

The jealous courtiers have discerned the minister's sympathy for the ascetics. When the king tests him, the minister rejoices and commends Junaysar's decision. The king does not reproach him, but the minister sees immediately that the king is displeased and he despairs. Then he remembers the man who claimed to mend words. He sends for him and explains his plight. The word-mender offers good counsel: the king thinks that the minister wishes to take his place, he explains. That is the tear that must be mended with the appropriate words. The minister should set aside his rich clothes and jewels, and put on the humble clothes of the ascetics, shave his head, and go to the king. He should tell Junaysar that he is ready to follow his friend and sovereign into the wilderness. The minister immediately follows the advice of the word-mender. When the king sees the sincerity of his minister's devotion to him, his suspicions are calmed and his trust in and favor for him increase. However, his anger toward the ascetics grows more intense. He exiles them from his country and kills all those who will not leave.

The story of the word-mender expands the description of the king's enmity toward the ascetic people of the Religion and, like the parables that will appear later in the narrative, it is probably based on an Arabic tale, though its source has not been clearly identified. It is an enduring addition to the story, perhaps because it introduces so well one of the themes that underlies the story: the conflict between loyalty to an earthly king and obedience to a spiritual lord.

## The Prince Leaves His Palace

The king's son Būdhāsaf grows into a young man. He longs to go out into the world and he wonders why his father has isolated him from it. He persuades Junaysar to allow him to venture into the city, but the king takes the precaution of ordering that any sign of misfortune or unhappiness must be hidden from the prince's view. However, one day as he rides through the city, Būdhāsaf encounters two beggars. One is diseased and the other is blind, and the prince sees illness and infirmity for the first time. Another day he sees an old man and learns that all living things must die. He then understands that the present world cannot offer salvation, and he turns to the ascetic life. King Junaysar attempts to engage his son in the pleasures of the world and the practice of his religion, but fails. The king's persecution of ascetics intensifies.

Although the Buddha's story is a clear source for the story of the king's son in the Arabic texts, the resemblance ends once the prince renounces his father's religion. The Arabic text then turns to a series of didactic exchanges about religion, first between the prince and his ascetic teacher, Bilawhar, then between the prince and his father. Apart from two short passages that may recall the Buddha's experience of sexual renunciation, one in each Arabic version of the story, the Buddha's story returns only at the end of the narrative in the account of Būdhāsaf's death.

The addition of Bilawhar, Būdhāsaf's teacher, may be the most significant change that the story undergoes as it is adopted into a Muslim context. One of the unique qualities of the Buddha in the Indian text is that he discovered the path to nirvana on his own, without relying on a teacher. After the Buddha leaves his palace, he studies with two teachers but soon discovers that they do not know the path to liberation. The monotheistic redactor of the Arabic text may have misunderstood the Buddha's relationship with the two masters whose doctrines he rejects, or he may have invented a teacher for Būdhāsaf in order to reconcile the edifying story of the Buddha with the belief that true knowledge is transmitted through a series of prophets (Moses, Jesus, Muhammad).[18] Whatever the origins of the prince's teacher, his importance in the story represents a significant modification and changes it into a succession of didactic lessons delivered in the form of parables.

## A Teacher Arrives

News of Prince Būdhāsaf's beauty, intelligence, and asceticism travels widely. The ascetic Bilawhar hears about the prince's renunciation of the world and vows to go "bring this living man out from among the dead." Bilawhar travels from Sarandīb (Ceylon) to teach him. He arrives disguised as a merchant and tells one of Būdhāsaf's servants that he has an exceedingly valuable jewel to offer the king's son: it will give sight to the blind, heal the sick, make the deaf hear and the weak strong; it protects against madness and vanquishes enemies. The servant marvels at the description of such a powerful object and asks to see the jewel before speaking about it to the prince. Bilawhar declines to reveal his merchandise. The servant's vision is weak, Bilawhar claims, and the jewel could blind him, but the prince has good sight and will be able to look upon it for as long as he likes. The courtier recounts Bilawhar's claims to Būdhāsaf, who immediately understands that Bilawhar has come to give him the wisdom he desires. The prince receives the ascetic, and Bilawhar begins to instruct Būdhāsaf in the Religion, teaching him to disdain the present world and look to the next and to heed the prophets who preach true wisdom.

Bilawhar's lessons are illustrated by parables and reinforced by maxims. He first teaches the prince the difference between worldly and spiritual values. He tells him about a pious king who worshipped the True God. One day, accompanied by his courtiers, the king met two poor men, barefoot and dressed in rags. The king dismounted, bowed before the wretched men, and embraced them. His courtiers denounced him for his lack of dignity and called on the king's brother to reproach him for forgetting his royal office by humbling himself before unworthy men. The brother went to the king and spoke the words he had prepared, but the king did not reply. A few days later the king sent a herald of death to sound his drum in front of his brother's door, a signal that he would be put to death. The following morning, the king's brother dressed himself in a shroud and went to the king's house, crying and lamenting. He threw himself before the king to beg for mercy. When the king asked him to explain his behavior, the brother cited the king's signal of his pending execution. The king corrected him: his brother was distraught because he had heard an order sounded by a herald. The king's brother should know that he had committed no crime for which the king would condemn him and yet he was still fearful. Moreover, the condemnation sounded by the herald came from a mortal man, not from his Creator. And yet, the king continued, his brother would blame him for bowing before the heralds of his own death, which he saw foreshadowed in the poor men he encountered on the road.

The king knew that his courtiers had led his brother astray, and he decided to teach them a lesson. He had four wooden caskets prepared. Two were filled with gold, silver, and gemstones but covered with black pitch on the outside. Another two caskets were covered with gold, but filled with filth. The king summoned his ministers, showed them the four caskets, and

asked which they thought were the most valuable. The courtiers responded quickly, identifying the two caskets covered in
gold as priceless; their importance and beauty should be obvious, they claimed. The insignificance and mediocrity of the
two caskets covered in pitch was equally obvious to the king's
courtiers, who judged them to have no value at all. The king
lifted the covers of the caskets his courtiers had judged worthless and showed them the riches they contained. These caskets are like the poor men they judged to be beneath them, he
explained. The courtiers judged the men by their appearance,
but beneath their poor exterior, they were filled with learning
and wisdom more valuable than the gold and gemstones in the
caskets. The king had the covers of the golden caskets lifted
and showed his ministers the filth inside. He explained that
these caskets were like the people who adorn themselves with
rich clothing and jewels but are filled with ignorance, resentment, envy, pride, and infamy. The king's ministers understood their error and recognized the worth of the men they
had disdained. So, too, Bilawhar says, Būdhāsaf has seen past
his poor exterior to the wisdom Bilawhar has brought him.

This parable and many more survive virtually unchanged
in the later *Barlaam and Josaphat* texts and in other works as
well; Shakespeare adapts the tale of the caskets in *The Merchant
of Venice. Bilawhar and Būdhāsaf* includes many more parables
than the later Christian versions of the story, and exchanges
among the characters are full of didactic examples. Both
Bilawhar and Būdhāsaf use parables in their conversations, the
king uses stories in debates with his son, and Būdhāsaf later
uses parables to teach others. In later versions of the story,

the didactic stories are increasingly reserved for the prince's teacher. All but two of the parables are found in the lessons of the teacher, Balawhar, in the Georgian version, and in subsequent versions, all but one parable is spoken by Barlaam. But in all versions of the story, the dialogue between the ascetic teacher and his disciple is structured in the form of questions and answers, and the teacher's answers often take the form of parables. They also include lengthy expositions of doctrine.

Bilawhar teaches Būdhāsaf that the Religion comes from God. Some will respond to His call, others will not, he explains; divine wisdom is available to some men but not to all. It is like the sun, Bilawhar says: some see its light, some are blind to it, and others see it imperfectly. This is why the Religion should only be preached to those capable of hearing and receiving it. Bilawhar recounts a parable about a king's courtier who heard and followed the words of divine wisdom. He shared everything with his king and told him all his thoughts, but he hesitated to declare his beliefs to his lord. The courtier consulted his friends about whether he should instruct the king, and they cautioned him to speak only if the king was worthy and would hear the truth. They warned that if he would not receive the truth, he could turn against the Religion and its practitioners. One evening the king and his courtier rode through the city and came upon a dung hill. Inside they saw an old, poor, and very ugly man dressed in rags, and they pitied him. Then they heard music, and they saw that the man was playing a guitar. His equally ugly wife, also dressed in rags, poured wine for him and danced as he played. The spouses praised each other's beauty, generosity, and nobility, demonstrating a contentment and gaiety that the king and his minister could not comprehend. In Bilawhar's parable, when the king expressed his surprise at the couple's pleasure in their poverty, his companion told him that from the perspective of the Eternal Kingdom, the king himself was a man rejoicing in poverty. The couple's joy is analogous to the pleasure of those who enjoy wealth and privilege in this world—they are all impoverished but do not see it; they enjoy their lives in this world and do not think of the next. The king reproached his minister for not telling him earlier about divine wisdom and commanded him to instruct him. The minister complied, and both men took "the path of salvation and deliverance."

All of Bilawhar's conversations with Būdhāsaf offer similar lessons: to heed the teaching of prophets, to disdain the pleasures of the present world, and to follow the ascetic life. The parables and sermons do not follow an obvious order, however. Indeed, the lack of a strong compositional logic in the ascetic's lessons persists in later versions of the story and may have contributed to the elimination or rearrangement of some of the parables as the story passed through further translations and rewritings.[19]

Bilawhar continues to teach the prince for four months, until one of Būdhāsaf's servants begins to worry about the wise man's frequent visits and goes to Būdhāsaf to express his concern that the king may not approve. Būdhāsaf persuades his servant to hide in his room and listen to the teaching of Bilawhar when he next comes to teach him. The servant hears Bilawhar's lessons and recognizes the wisdom of his words, but he fears the king's anger should he discover Bilawhar's presence and asks Būdhāsaf what he should do. The prince counsels his servant to keep his secret, but the servant fears betraying the king's trust. He pretends to be ill and does not return to Būdhāsaf's palace. At this time, Bilawhar decides to leave Būdhāsaf to return to his hermitage. Būdhāsaf wishes to accompany him, but Bilawhar forbids it: the prince's departure would bring the king's wrath upon the ascetics. He would do better to remain at his father's court and convince him to abandon his persecution of the people of the Religion. Bilawhar takes his leave of Būdhāsaf, and the king's son worships God in secret, spending his nights in prayer.

## The King Tries to Keep His Son

The departure of Bilawhar marks the end of the first part of the story. In the longer version of *Bilawhar and Būdhāsaf*, our focus here, the second part of the story recounts a series of exchanges between Būdhāsaf and his father and other defenders of idolatry (the shorter version of the story omits these debates). As the story continues, King Junaysar learns that one of the courtiers he placed in Būdhāsaf's household has fallen ill and sends his own physician to heal him. The doctor cannot discover any illness and reports to Junaysar that the courtier must suffer from some anxiety, for he is in good health. The king fears that his man has angered Būdhāsaf somehow, and the prince's displeasure causes him to suffer. He sends word that he will visit the courtier the next day, but before the king can leave his palace, the man rises, dresses, and goes to meet the king. He explains that his illness comes from his heart, but he still does not dare to tell the king about Būdhāsaf's secret conversion, so he attributes his debilitating concern to a dream. The courtier recounts that while he slept he saw a crowd descend on a grove of trees and destroy them all. In their place grew a single great tree that then left the grove and came to Būdhāsaf. As the king's son sat at the foot of the tree and listened to it, the tree shook its branches and its leaves fell into Būdhāsaf's ears and passed into his belly, and his belly grew. Then the tree left, and Būdhāsaf himself became a tree, taller and more beautiful than the first tree. In the dream, Junaysar arrived with a great crowd of people and approached the tree. The tree shook its branches and the leaves fell on the king and those who accompanied him, but after the leaves fell to the ground they flew back up onto the branches from which they had fallen. After the king and his people left, others assembled around the tree, and its leaves fell into their ears. Each of them became a tree in turn, and the grove was filled with trees, more beautiful than it had been before.

The king does not respond to the courtier's recital of his dream, but ponders its meaning. He sends for an interpreter of dreams named Rākis, who reveals to the king that what his courtier recounted was not a dream but a vision. Junaysar confronts the courtier, and the man explains that the invented dream represented both what he had seen and what he had divined about the future. He then tells the king about Bilawhar's visits to his son.

King Junaysar is overcome by anger and devises a plan with the astrologer Rākis. They will capture Bilawhar and make him renounce his beliefs. When the prince sees that

Bilawhar cannot defend his Religion, he will turn away from asceticism and return to his father's idolatrous religion. If they cannot find Bilawhar, Rākis will use his magic charms to take on the ascetic's appearance. He will pretend to be Būdhāsaf's teacher and enter into a formal disputation with the king's wise men, who will defend the idolaters' religion. Rākis, disguised as Bilawhar, will allow himself to be defeated and he will renounce his beliefs. Rākis promises the king that Būdhāsaf will follow his teacher's example.

Junaysar sends his men out to search for Bilawhar. They do not find him, but come upon a group of ascetics, led by a man carrying human bones tied to a cord. The ascetics refuse to tell the king's men where they can find Bilawhar; they will not reveal his whereabouts even when threatened with death. In fact, the ascetics ask their captors why they should fear death. Life in this world holds no attraction or pleasure for them. The king's men take their captives back to court, where the king claims that the ascetics will become bones like those they carry if they do not reveal Bilawhar's location. The man who carries them replies that they keep the bones out of veneration for those who have suffered and died because of the king's persecutions, and as a reminder that death waits for all men. They do not lament for the dead, but for those still living; they will happily add their bones to those they carry. Next, the ascetics reproach the king for his persecutions of ascetics, and he condemns them to be tortured and killed.

Rākis then disguises himself as Bilawhar and the king pretends to capture and imprison him. Before resorting to the staged debate, the king tries to bring Būdhāsaf back to his faith

by reminding his son of the loyalty he owes to his father and
to his lineage. Būdhāsaf responds to each of his father's claims
for the superiority of his own faith and to each of his criticisms
of his son's faith. Just as the king, like Bilawhar before him,
uses parables to illustrate his claims, so too Būdhāsaf uses parables to refute his father's claims. One of these is a story about
*al-Budd*.

## The Prophet al-Budd

Al-Budd appears only in the debates between Būdhāsaf and
his father. When the king reproaches and threatens Būdhāsaf
because he will not worship idols, the prince explains that
al-Budd brought the word of God to the Indians and later
died as he journeyed through that land. The 'Anqā, a mythical
bird, found his corpse and carried it away to feed its young.
Because of the virtuous life lived by al-Budd, when the young
birds consumed his body they were filled with piety, goodness, sincerity, knowledge, and wisdom. The young bird that
ate al-Budd's eyes saw the vanity of the world; the one that
ate his ears heard the cries of the poor and the lessons of the
sages; the one that ate his nose rejected the odors of the world;
the one that ate his tongue could not bear the bitter taste of a
lie; and the one that ate his heart felt what all the others felt,
for what was divided among them was held in the heart. The
bird that ate the heart gained knowledge of the future life and
became a guide for his siblings, telling them about al-Budd
and his lessons. Together the young birds agreed to reject their
present life in order to seek a future one. When their parent
returned, bringing them prey, they divided it among them-

selves, then took the nourishment into the desert and threw it away. When they became thin and the 'Anqā asked why, the young bird that ate al-Budd's tongue explained that once they had been nourished from al-Budd's body, they had no need of further sustenance. They refused this life in anticipation of the next. When the 'Anqā threatened to beat the young birds, they were not afraid and welcomed the chance to pass more quickly into the next life. The 'Anqā then killed its young, which is why it disappeared from the world and can no longer be seen. Būdhāsaf tells his father that he is like the 'Anqā's young. Like them, he welcomes his father's punishment, for he no longer cares for this world and longs only for the next. King Junaysar understands that his reproaches will have no effect on his son. He leaves Būdhāsaf and returns to his own palace, full of sorrow and regret.

Al-Budd appears only in the long version of *Bilawhar and Būdhāsaf*; in the shorter version the entire debate between the king and his son is absent. The introduction of al-Budd may be a later addition to the original form of the story, but if it is an interpolation, it appears to have been a very early one. Both Būdhāsaf and King Junaysar cite al-Budd as an authority for their beliefs, and both father and son claim to be disciples of al-Budd as they dispute the nature of the good and the truth of their respective religions. Both claim to follow the true teachings of al-Budd: For King Junaysar, the prophet taught charity and goodness but did not require the renunciation of the world. For Būdhāsaf, al-Budd preached the renunciation of the earthly world, the very renunciation practiced by the ascetics whom his father persecutes.

After his father leaves him, Būdhāsaf goes to visit the

ascetics taken prisoner during the search for Bilawhar. They have been tortured and most of them have died; only the bone carrier and two others survive. Būdhāsaf strips off his clothes, has his men tie his hands behind his back, and walks among the ascetics lamenting their fate. The man who carries the bones of the dead speaks to Būdhāsaf and tells him that those he laments have suffered at the hands of powerful men, but their souls do not feel bodily pain. They have gone to join their Master and receive the rewards he will bestow. Būdhāsaf tells the suffering ascetics that he is the king's son and he confesses his fear that his own conversion has provoked the king's violence. He asks them to confirm his path in the ascetic religion by releasing his bound hands. The three suffering men rejoice that although King Junaysar has destroyed their bodies, they can still use their tongues. They praise God and claim that the king's violence has only increased their compassion toward the prince's father. They bless Būdhāsaf and exhort him to use his freedom and his office to promote and strengthen the Religion of God. They pray that God will pardon his sins and release his hands, and Būdhāsaf's bound hands are miraculously freed. The ascetics encourage the prince in his resolve to leave the world and its pleasures. Būdhāsaf embraces the bone carrier and stays with the dying men until their souls leave their bodies. Then he buries them.

The figure of the ascetic bone carrier appears in the later Christian versions of the story, in which the bones he carries are easily identified as saints' relics. But Būdhāsaf's confession to the dying ascetics, his plea for their forgiveness, and their confirmation of the path he has chosen are elements of the Arabic story that drop out of the later versions, perhaps because of the expanded role of the prince's teacher, Barlaam, in leading the prince toward a formal conversion and baptism, and in exhorting him to his faith.

## The King Reminds His Son of His Lineage

King Junaysar learns of his son's departure from the palace and sets out to find him, bringing forty leaders of the idolaters to dispute Būdhāsaf's beliefs, forty witches to cast him out of his madness, and forty noble princes to remind him of his office and noble heritage. The king finds his son praying in front of the cave where he has buried the tortured ascetics. Junaysar reasons with Būdhāsaf and tries to convince him that his nature should incline him toward the idolatrous religion of his father and forefathers. Būdhāsaf's ancestor Baysam was the first disciple of al-Budd, King Junaysar reminds his son, and he claims that the teachings of al-Budd do not require him to renounce the ties of lineage. Būdhāsaf rejects his father's claim that he can serve al-Budd while enjoying the privileges of his office, and he rejects the notion that loyalty to his lineage is more important than loyalty to his beliefs. To prove his point, he tells a parable recounted by al-Budd.

A man approached al-Budd as he rested under a tree. He explained that his brother had chosen to leave the world, abandoning his aged parents and young siblings, while he himself chose to stay with his family and support them until the parents died and his siblings grew up. He asked al-Budd which brother was closer to the truth. Al-Budd replied with a parable.

The young sons of a king became separated from their father in the middle of a desert. The two boys took refuge in a cave where a group of monkeys lived. The monkeys treated the children with kindness, and the boys decided to stay with them because, they reasoned, there are none among all the wild animals that resemble humans so closely or that are more gentle, useful, and well disposed toward them. The boys stayed with the monkeys until they reached puberty, and the animals treated them as members of their species. The female monkeys seduced the boys, and the boys slept with them and fathered children. Over the years the king continued to search for his lost sons, and when he finally learned where to find them, he sent messengers bearing presents and leading horses that would carry them back to their father. One brother was eager to return to his father's kingdom, but the other boy's attachment to the place, his children, and his animal spouses, as well as his fear of the long journey across the desert, caused him to stay with the monkeys.

Al-Budd then asked his interlocutor which brother was closer to the truth. The man asked in bewilderment how al-Budd could compare his relationship with his family to the relationship between the boys and the monkeys. Al-Budd replied that the bodies of men are more like the bodies of monkeys than they are like those of our spiritual relations. Spiritual kinship is the only true lineage, and it can be attained only through the rejection of the body, he explained. Būdhāsaf uses the story to illustrate that spiritual attachment should take priority over blood relations, and he claims to have learned this lesson from al-Budd.

Būdhāsaf argues that his father's words honor al-Budd, but his actions contradict the prophet's teachings. He recounts other parables to show his father that to follow al-Budd means renouncing the world of privilege, wealth, and position and looking to the next world for rewards. King Junaysar is almost persuaded by his son's preaching, but then he remembers the comforts of his life and the pleasures he enjoys, and he resists the truths that Būdhāsaf would teach him. He remembers the ruse planned by Rākis and proposes to his son that they test their faiths in a disputation. He will proclaim amnesty for the ascetics so that they may attend, and he will assemble his priests and wise men to debate with Bilawhar. The king's son agrees.

## The King Neglects His Idols

On the chosen day, people assemble from throughout the kingdom. High priests gather to dispute their religion with Bilawhar, represented by the disguised Rākis. None of the ascetics attend the disputation, and only one believer in the Religion is present to take Bilawhar's side. The king and his son each agree that if his faith is proven wrong, he will convert to the other's religion. King Junaysar then addresses the idolatrous priests. If they are defeated, he vows, he will destroy all his idols and give up his crown. Moreover, he will kill all his priests, enslave their wives, and crucify their children. Būdhāsaf likewise addresses Rākis, who has used magic charms to take the form of Bilawhar. He vows that if the disguised Rākis is bested by the priests of idolatry, he will rip out his heart and his tongue and feed them to dogs. Rākis sees that his ruse has turned against him and that he will die if he does not successfully defend the Religion. He begins eloquently to deny the power of idols and to defend the ascetics and their faith. The king is enraged to see Rākis defend the Religion so well, but he cannot speak to him without revealing the deception they planned together.

At the end of the day, Rākis has defeated the king's philosophers in debate, and Būdhāsaf takes him back to his palace. The prince reveals that he knows that Rākis is not Bilawhar. The prince exhorts Rākis to believe his own arguments and convinces him of the truth of the words he himself used to defend the ascetics' beliefs. Rākis undoes his spell and resumes his own form and appearance. He reveals to Būdhāsaf that his father the king will live for only two more years and encourages the prince to live with him in filial piety until he dies. Rākis converts to the Religion and leaves Būdhāsaf to go into the wilderness and live as an ascetic. Junaysar recognizes that his plan to deceive his son has failed, and the king loses faith in his idols. Although he does not convert to the Religion, he abandons his efforts to persuade his son to return to idolatry.

Meanwhile, the priests are concerned by the king's neglect of his idols. A great feast day approaches and King Junaysar has made none of his usual preparations for the celebration. The priests seek to revive the king's support for their religion and they turn to a *bahwan*, an idolater who lives in the wilderness like the ascetics but does not share their beliefs.[20] First the *bahwan* persuades the king to celebrate the feast day for his idols. Then to reward Junaysar's demonstration of his faith, he tells him how he can win his son back to his religion: the king must call on demons to help him, for they will be powerful allies against his son. When the king asks how demons can be enlisted in his cause, the *bahwan* uses a parable to explain.

The *bahwan*'s parable sounds very much like Būdhāsaf's own story. A much desired son was born to a king and when the king assembled his astrologers to foretell the prince's future, the wise men announced that the prince would die if he saw the sun before his tenth birthday. The king had a great pit excavated and furnished with everything his son could need, and he closed his son inside along with his nurses, servants, and teachers. The child stayed in the pit for ten years, and he was then released. His father had him taken through the city and commanded that all things be brought out and displayed for the child so that he could see them and learn their names. All kinds of animals, trees, and goods were shown to the boy, and as he saw them he asked their names. He passed by women and asked what they were called. Those accompanying him replied that these beings were demons who seduced men and led them astray. The prince was filled with love and admiration for them, and when he returned to the king and his father asked him what had most pleased him, the boy replied that of all he saw, the demons pleased him most. And so, the *bahwan* concludes, women are the demons that can help King Junaysar win his son.

Junaysar immediately has all the male servants removed from Būdhāsaf's palace and replaces them with four thousand of the most beautiful women in the country. He charges the women to care for Būdhāsaf, to love and entice him, and the women comply. They wear seductive clothing or no clothes at all; they speak sweetly to the prince; they sing and play music; they accompany him on outings; they even debate with him about the truth of his religion. Among the women is a princess more beautiful and learned than all the others. Būdhāsaf is drawn to her and speaks with her frequently, trying to convince her to abandon idolatry and devote herself to the Religion. She bargains with the king's son: if he will become her lover for a year, at the end of the year she will adopt his religion and live chastely with him for the rest of their lives. Būdhāsaf will not agree. The lady then proposes that he spend a month with her, or just a single night. Būdhāsaf is no more immune to the seductions of women than any other man, the narrator tells us, and he is tempted. Satan enters his body and convinces him to surrender to his desire; the prince spends a single night with the lady and she conceives a son. Afterward, Būdhāsaf regrets his actions.

When the king learns of the princess's pregnancy, he is delighted because he thinks that his lineage is now assured, since his grandson will inherit his throne if his son will not take it. King Junaysar no longer depends on the women to convince Būdhāsaf to return to idolatry, but he keeps them in his son's palace. Satan continues to torment Būdhāsaf with the women's beauty, and the prince seeks refuge in prayer. One night while he lies prostrate in devotion to God, his soul is taken from his body. He sees Bilawhar and the bone carrier coming toward him. They take him to Paradise, where he sees a brilliant splendor unlike any he has seen on earth. He compares the lowliest things of Paradise to the most beautiful women from his palace, and the women appear repugnant to

him. Bilawhar and the bone carrier show him the place that
awaits him in Paradise, and they then return his soul to his
body. Būdhāsaf awakes and sees the women gathered around
him; they saw his still and unbreathing body and feared he had
died. Būdhāsaf gazes on the women and is filled with disgust
for them.

The king's effort to use the seductions of women to bring
his son back to his religion draws on an episode from the life
of the Buddha and is also found in all subsequent versions of
the story, but sexual attraction is only one of the attachments
to the world that the prince rejects. Unlike the hero of the later
Christian versions of the story, Būdhāsaf does not remain a
virgin, and virginity and chastity do not assume the central
place that they hold in *Barlaam and Josaphat*. In this regard, the
Arabic text more closely resembles the story of the Buddha,
who also produces an heir before he renounces the world.

## Būdhāsaf Preaches the Religion

King Junaysar learns of the change in his son and goes to visit
him. Būdhāsaf tells his father about his vision of Paradise and
calls on him to serve God and His Religion. He reminds him
of the prophecy that foretold his death: the king has but a short
time left to live and he has no hope of joining his ancestors
in a future life if he does not put his faith in God's Religion.
Būdhāsaf assures his father that even though he has been
imperfect in this life, his conversion would assure his comfort and contentment in the future life. The king is moved and
wishes to turn to God. He embraces the Religion and aban-

dons his idols. Junaysar sends the women out of Būdhāsaf's palace and dwells there with his son.

After the king renounces idolatry, his subjects also neglect the idols. The *bahwan* comes to Būdhāsaf to reproach him for abandoning his ancestral gods and preventing his people from worshipping their true gods. Būdhāsaf reasons with the *bahwan*, teaching him about the difference between appearance and reality, and argues that the *bahwan*'s gods offer only the appearance of truth and power, whereas al-Budd reveals the true word of God. Būdhāsaf convinces the *bahwan* to renounce idolatry and embrace asceticism. The *bahwan*'s conversion is a final blow to the idolaters. Their priests are scattered, and the people openly distrust them.

Būdhāsaf's son is born, and after the child's birth, his mother keeps her promise to live chastely until her death. The king keeps his grandson close to him, but he regrets that he has such a short time to live and fears that without his protection, the young boy will not inherit his kingdom. The king questions wise men about his grandson's future. Unlike the astrologers who predicted his son's renunciation of his kingdom, they confirm that the king's lineage will prosper; his grandson will have a long life and many descendants. The king is content and happy that he heeded Būdhāsaf's urgings to follow the Religion.

*Būdhāsaf and Bilawhar* ends with an account of Būdhāsaf's death that clearly draws on the life of the Buddha. An angel from God goes to Būdhāsaf and tells him that it is time to leave this world to seek the kingdom that will never end. Būdhāsaf should prepare himself, for the angel will come to summon him shortly. Būdhāsaf does not speak of the angel's visit, nor does he announce his departure, but he is prepared when the angel arrives in the night. He goes to the palace gate and asks for his horse. A young man runs after him and reproaches him for leaving. His people have long anticipated his reign, the man claims, and they have desired to live under his rule. Būdhāsaf sends the young man home and tells him that if he will help the prince leave his kingdom, he will have a share in all that he accomplishes after his departure. Būdhāsaf mounts his horse and prepares to leave, but then changes his mind and dismounts to go on foot, telling his squire to take the horse back to his parents. His squire asks how he will tell Būdhāsaf's parents of his departure. He regrets the prince's decision and the hard life of solitude he has chosen. Būdhāsaf's horse also regrets his decision. It bows before the prince and kisses his feet. God gives the horse speech and it begs Būdhāsaf not to leave it behind, but the prince is resolved to depart alone. He gives his rich clothing, his jewels, and his horse to his servant, then travels north on foot until he reaches a great plain. Near a spring he sees a tree full of birds and takes it as a symbol of his mission. Four angels take him to heaven and reveal everything there to him, and then Būdhāsaf returns to his native land. His father learns of his arrival and comes to meet him with honor. Būdhāsaf preaches the Religion to the people and the land is full of wisdom. The day of King Junaysar's death arrives, and Būdhāsaf stays with him.

These episodes share much in common with the story of the Buddha. On the night that Prince Siddhārtha renounces the world, he leaves the palace on his royal steed Kaṇṭhaka accompanied by his groom Chandaka. Once outside the city he exchanges his royal dress for the common clothes of Chandaka and sends him back to inform his father of his departure. He also bids farewell to his horse, which dies of a broken heart. After six years of ascetic practice, he finds the Bodhi Tree and sits down under it, meditating all night and achieving enlightenment at dawn. Now the Buddha, he gathers a group of disciples, eventually returning to the capital, where he teaches the *dharma* to his father. His teaching is not represented as an effort to convert, but simply as a sharing of the truth that the Buddha has come to understand. Unlike the Arabic tale, the Buddha's father does not die at that time and the Buddha's young son does not become heir to the throne; instead, he becomes a monk. Later, hearing that his father is dying, the Buddha flies through the sky to be with him, and then preaches to him so that his father can attain enlightenment and enter nirvana.

In *Bilawhar and Būdhāsaf*, the prince buries Junaysar according to the custom of the ascetics. Then he assembles all his relatives and the princes of the realm and calls them to the Religion of God, and they embrace it. He destroys the idols and transforms their temples into places for the worship of God. He converts all the people of the land, and thirty thousand of them become ascetics who renounce the world to live in the wilderness. The prince chooses his uncle Samṭā as his successor, and then he leaves his land to wander through the cities of India calling people to the Religion of God.

When he arrives finally at Kashmir, it is time for him to die. He gives his last counsel to his disciple, Abābid, and the people of Kashmir. He says, "I have taught, protected, and raised up the Church, I have put there the lamps of those who came

before me, I have reassembled the dispersed flock of Islam
to which I was sent. Now the moment comes when I will be
raised out of this world and my spirit will be freed from its
body. Observe your commandments, do not stray from the
truth, adopt the ascetic life! Let Ababid be your leader!" We
hear in this speech echoes of the final instructions of the Buddha, who told his monks to be a lamp (or island) unto themselves and to strive for their salvation. However, significantly,
the Buddha does not appoint a successor, telling his monks that
his teachings would be their teacher after he is gone.

Būdhāsaf then orders Ababid to smooth a place for him on
the ground. He lies down on his side, stretches out his legs,
and points his head toward the north. This scene also appears
in the life of the Buddha. At the time of his death, the Buddha, accompanied by his disciple Ānanda, went into a forest.
He lay down between two trees with his head pointing north
and, after giving his final instructions, passed into nirvana.
Būdhāsaf turns his face toward the east and then he dies.

Būdhāsaf's uncle Samṭā succeeds him as ruler of the land of
Sūlābaṭ, and after his death Šāmil, son of Būdhāsaf, rules the
land according to his father's religion. He has many descendants, and they all rule according to the Right Path.

### The Buddha, al-Budd, and Bilawhar

The Buddha figures twice in *Bilawhar and Būdhāsaf*—as a
holy prophet, al-Budd, whom both Būdhāsaf and his father
claim to follow, and as the protagonist, Būdhāsaf, whose life
resembles that of the Buddha, at least at its beginning and end.

The translator-compiler most likely used a Persian translation of the life of the Buddha as a frame for the collection of parables and exemplary stories. References to the prophet called al-Budd allow for a secondary frame: both Būdhāsaf and King Junaysar retell parables told by al-Budd. Such a structure is not unique to *Bilawhar and Būdhāsaf*, and indeed, frame narratives are a well-known Arabic literary genre in this period. The example closest to *Bilawhar and Būdhāsaf* may be the *Pañcatantra*, a collection of Indian stories enclosed within a frame when they were translated into Arabic. Other examples include *The Book of Sinbad* and *A Thousand and One Nights*. In *Bilawhar and Būdhāsaf* the framed stories have a didactic purpose, which is why they are usually referred to as parables or apologues. In this respect, *Bilawhar and Būdhāsaf* is similar to the widespread genre of wisdom literature, collections of sayings and maxims intended to teach eloquence and compositional skills to administrative secretaries and court intellectuals.

Composed during the Abbasid caliphate at a time when the capital of the Islamic empire had shifted from Damascus to Baghdad and Persian texts were being translated into Arabic, *Bilawhar and Būdhāsaf* represents an intercultural grappling with difference. It brings a story about India and religion to a Muslim Arabic culture, and it seems to explore shared rather than different values. But if the translation of the Buddha's story into Arabic and into a context compatible with Islam seems to suggest commonalities, it may also suggest difference. Extant copies of *Bilawhar and Būdhāsaf* are associated with Shi'a Muslims, who represented a minority under the

Sunni Abbasid caliphate. It may be that the story of the persecuted people of the Religion had added meaning for Shi'a minority sects, and that *Bilawhar and Būdhāsaf* was treasured not just for its moral and ethical lessons, but also for the story of spiritual triumph it recounts.

# CHAPTER THREE

# The Prince Becomes a Christian Saint: The Georgian *Balavariani*

Not long after the Buddha was transformed into Būdhāsaf, Georgian monks in Palestine turned the tale of the prince into the story of a saintly son who eventually converts his idolater father. Why would the Georgian monks select this particular story to Christianize, a story they must have read in Arabic? Many have argued that the story of the anonymous Buddha is so compelling to any who read it—in any language and in any historical age—that it must be repeated. But there may have also been reasons that were less ethereal and more firmly grounded in Christian Palestine.

It is perhaps no coincidence that *Barlaam and Ioasaph* was long thought to have been translated into Greek by a famous monk in Palestine. After the conversion of the Roman emperor Constantine in 315 CE, Jerusalem was rebuilt as a Christian city. Formerly a provincial outpost, it became one of the most important cities in the Roman empire and a major pilgrimage site for Christians from the Byzantine empire and the Christian West. Jerusalem was conquered by Muslims in 628 and held until the city was won by Christians in 1099 during the First Crusade. Even under Muslim rule, Jerusalem was the center of the world for medieval Christians, and the city appeared quite literally at the center of medieval maps, where geographical logic situated the entire world around the holy city.

Palestine was the site of many Christian monastic communities, some established as early as the mid-fourth century, and in the following centuries, many more were founded. According to one source, in 516 as many as ten thousand monks dwelled in Jerusalem and the surrounding desert.[1] The Persian and Arab invasions of the seventh century disrupted monastic life in Palestine but did not end it, and many monastic foundations survived under the Muslim conquest. Among them was St. Sabas, where a certain John composed *Barlaam and Ioasaph*, according to an early manuscript copy of the story.

Despite its Buddhist or Muslim contexts, the story of ascetic renunciation must have had an immediate resonance for Christians, especially Christian monks. The ascetics engaged in spiritual exercises in the wilderness would remind any medieval Christian of the Desert Fathers, men (and a few women) who, beginning in the third century CE, left society to devote themselves to God and lived in great privation and isolation in Egypt and Syria. The most famous of these Christian ascetics was Saint Anthony. He was born in Herakleopolis in Lower Egypt. When Anthony was eighteen, his parents died, leaving him their estate and responsibility for his sister. Around 270, he heard a sermon on Matthew 19:21, where Jesus says, "If you wish to be perfect, go and sell your possessions and give the money to the poor, and you will have treasure in heaven; then come, follow me." He did so, selling his estate, giving the money to the poor, and placing his sister in a nunnery. He then left the city and went into the Egyptian desert, where he renounced the demands of the body to devote himself entirely to God, enduring many hardships and temptations. Like the ascetics in our story, then, some Christians left the secular world to live in an untamed domain. The desire to leave the world was motivated not so much by the desire to escape persecution, as by the choice to care for the soul rather than the body. By the time of Anthony's death in 356, more than a thousand monks and nuns were living in the desert. This was the beginning of Christian monasticism.

It was in this milieu that the pious prince's ultimate triumph over his idolatrous father would be rewritten by the Georgian monks translating the Arabic story not simply as the triumph of Christianity, but also as a triumph of Christian monasticism. The Arabic story could then be used to give an account of Christian history and, in particular, of the triumph of Christian asceticism over an idolatrous king who persecuted Christians. For the Georgian translators, a no less sinister idolatrous king was part of their own history.

In 327, at the time of the emperor Constantine, Mirian III of Iberia made Christianity the state religion. (Iberia is the name given by the Greeks and Romans to the eastern and southern regions of what is today Georgia.) Later, during the fifth century, Iberia was largely under the control of the Persian Sassanid empire, although it remained a land claimed by Persia and Byzantium until Muslim armies moved through the area. In 645 Iberia became a tributary state of the Islamic Empire. The Christian community was not forced to convert, but those who refused to adopt Islam had to pay the hated jizya, a tax that Islamic law required from all able-bodied males who remained unbelievers. The Christian princes of Iberia led a series of unsuccessful revolts in protest, leading to further persecution.

Most Georgians remained Christians, and the most pious among them left Iberia and traveled to Palestine, where they established monasteries in the vicinity of Jerusalem beginning in the sixth century. One of the most famous is the Monastery of Saint Sabas (known as Mar Saba in Arabic), where translators and copyists produced many texts. The Arabic *Bilawhar and Būdhāsaf* may have been translated into Georgian there, since the monastery is mentioned by name in several manuscripts of the Greek version of the tale.

The Muslim conquest of Iberia continued into the eighth century. In 735, troops under the command of the general (and future caliph) Marwan ibn Muhammad (688–750), remembered in Georgia as "Marwan the Deaf," invaded the region, bringing it under control after two years of bloody fighting. The emirate of Tblisi was established in 736 and would rule the region until the city was recaptured by the Christian king Davit IV in 1122.

In Georgia, Marwan is remembered for his ruthlessness, particularly involving the death of two Christian princes, the brothers Davit and Constantine Mkheidze, who led their troops into battle against the Muslim army. They repulsed the advance once but were defeated and taken prisoner in a second

battle. When they were brought before Marwan, they defi-
antly told him, "Your laughter and boasting are in vain, since
earthly glory is fleeting and soon fades away. It is not your
valor that has captured us but our own sins. For the atonement
of our sins we have fallen into the hands of the godless enemy."
Impressed by their forbearance when they were tortured, Marwan promised to spare them if they would convert to Islam,
but Constantine replied, "My brother Davit and I believe and
follow the one faith and one doctrine in which we have been
instructed. Our faith is in the Father and the Son and the Holy
Spirit, and we will die for the sake of the One True God."[2]
Marwan then enlisted the aid of sorcerers to make the brothers
convert. When this failed, Marwan had the brothers starved for
ten days and then thrown into a river with stones tied around
their necks. Their bodies floated free and were recovered by
Christians, who hid the brothers in a cave. Centuries later,
King Bagrat the Great (1072–1117) was hunting in the region
when he is said to have discovered the uncorrupted bodies of
the brothers, bathed in light. He had Motsameta Monastery,
the Monastery of the Martyrs, built to house their relics, which
have been credited over the centuries with many miraculous
healings.

It was during this period of turmoil that our story was
translated from Arabic into Georgian and then into Greek by
the Georgian monks in Jerusalem. Once the Arabic *Bilawhar
and Būdhāsaf* was translated and Christianized in the Georgian *Balavariani*, the shape of the story was set for centuries. It
would be modified in its particulars and some episodes would
be rearranged, but the story's plot and the parables it includes,
all taken from the Arabic version, remained consistent as the

story made its way from Georgian into Greek, then into Latin, and subsequently into virtually every European vernacular language.

The *Balavariani*, the earliest Georgian version of our story, was composed in the ninth or tenth century. An abridged version of the story, translated and published as *The Wisdom of Balahvar*, was composed later, perhaps as late as the eleventh century. We discuss the longer version here since it will be the source for the next link in the transmission chain, the Greek *Barlaam and Ioasaph*.

## The Idolatrous King and the Christian Hermit

The Georgian *Balavariani* is divided into three books. Book I begins in India in a place called Sholait (Sūlābaṭ in Arabic) ruled by a fierce and terrible pagan king, here called Abenes. He has long hated and persecuted Christians, yet their number grows in his land. The ascetic Christians disapprove of the king's pursuit of worldly pleasures and constantly proclaim the faults of this transitory world. Fearing a revolt, the king arrests and tortures Christians and increases his offerings to idols. Otherwise, the king is generally content in his life. There is only one thing he lacks: a son who would be his heir.

The king is distraught when one of his favorite knights becomes a Christian and renounces the world, leaving the city to live in the wilderness with the ascetics. He summons the man, and when the knight appears dressed in rags like a hermit, King Abenes scolds him for making a mockery of the honors he had received. The king tells the knight that he will be judged and punished just like anyone else who has committed a crime. The knight agrees to submit to the king's will—although he does not know what crime he has committed—if the king will agree to judge him with wisdom and not wrath. The king agrees and asks the man to explain why he has left his position and privileges at court to join the Christians.

The knight quotes a saying that he heard often in his youth: "The fool imagines the real thing to be unreal, and mistakes the unreal for the real. Whoever fails to comprehend the real thing will be unable to cast out what is unreal."[3] The knight explains that "the real" names the world to come and "the unreal," this present world. He contemplated this saying over the years, he says, and eventually came to see the world as a furnace of fire. No longer ensnared by his worldly passions, he set his eyes on the future life. He saw the shortcomings of the transitory world; he understood that what appears to be pure is in reality corrupt, that joy is sorrow, that wealth is poverty, and that exaltation is debasement. All the things that bring pleasure—whether property or children or good health—immediately become causes of anxiety because of the fear of losing them. Today the world offers a man a great banquet; tomorrow it turns him into a feast for worms. The knight says that those who are most endowed with worldly riches should be the first to see them as a prison and renounce the world. They should place their faith in the eternity of heaven promised by God. After hearing this long speech, the king responds that the knight should die for his beliefs and that he spares his life only because he promised he would allow the knight to speak freely. However, the king increases his persecution of the Christians and his support of the pagan priests.

The beginning of the Georgian story is much like the opening of *Bilawhar and Būdhāsaf*, and like the Arabic text, the *Balavariani* follows the Buddha's story in its description of the birth of the king's much desired son, though the prophetic dream of the prince's mother is absent. In fact, the prince's mother does not appear in the *Balavariani* or in any of the subsequent medieval translations. In the Georgian version, as in the Arabic, a handsome son is born to the king. Abenes names him Iodasaph and praises the idols for this great gift. He gathers the court astrologers to predict the prince's future, and they agree that he will become the greatest king in India. However, the wisest among them specifies that the child's glory will not be in this world, and he claims that the prince will be a great guide on the road to truth. Alarmed at this prospect, the king has a special palace built for his son. His every pleasure is indulged; the servants are replaced when they begin to grow old, and anyone who is sick is removed; death, disease, and eternity may not be mentioned in his presence. "All these measures the king took so as to prevent the prince from seeing anything which might give him cause for wonderment, and thus lead him to make enquiry about the faith of the Christians." He also banished all the Christians. When the king encounters two hermits leaving his land, he has them burned to death. This inspires the idolaters to attack and kill the priests and monks living in the wilderness, until there are no practicing Christians left in the land apart from those hiding in catacombs and those afraid to profess their faith openly. Christianity becomes a memory.

The king's son grows into an intelligent and handsome young man and he begins to resent his inability to leave the palace. He wonders why his father will not allow him to find out for himself what is right and wrong. He asks his trusted tutor to tell him the reason for his confinement. The tutor tells him about the wise man's prophecy and about the Christians and their virtues. The prince then confronts his father and claims that he suffers because he cannot see what lies outside the palace gates. The king agrees to allow his son to ride outside the palace walls, but orders the prince's escorts to take him only to beautiful places and to avoid the sight of anything unpleasant. One day while out riding, the prince and his servants encounter a crippled man and a blind man walking together. When their affliction is explained to him, the prince asks if all men will suffer such a fate. He is told that only some are so afflicted, but no one can know who will suffer and who will be spared. Later they see an old man. The prince asks when people must die, and his companions reply that most men live eighty or a hundred years, and the prince asks what a year is and then what a month is. When he learns that all who live in the world are subject to sickness and death, no matter how noble or brave they may be, the prince becomes deeply grieved: "No longer is there any sweetness in this transitory life now that I have seen these things; and no one has any respite from sudden or gradual death." The prince feigns happiness before his father, but summons his tutor to ask if there are any who follow a different faith. He learns that there used to be Christians in the land, people who hate this world and seek an eternal kingdom, but the king has banished them all. Iodasaph comes to detest the world and his discontent becomes known beyond the walls of the palace.

As Book II begins, news of the prince reaches a pious monk named Balahvar living in the land of Sarandib (Sarandīb, the Arabic name for Sri Lanka, is the source of the English word "serendipity"). He sails to India disguised as a merchant and proceeds to court, where he meets Iodasaph's tutor. He tells the prince's companion that he has brought a hidden treasure of great value, one capable of curing diseases, granting victory over enemies, and driving out demons. However, it only has these powers for those whose eyes are clear and whose bodies are without sin, like Prince Iodasaph; it will harm anyone else. When Prince Iodasaph learns of the treasure Balahvar brings he summons the hermit, who promises to show it to him only after testing his worth. Balahvar then relates a series of thirteen fables in response to questions and requests from Iodasaph. The hermit's stories convey Christian truths, and the prince comes to believe them and wishes to convert. Balahvar relates the parable about the sower of seeds (drawn from Matthew 13) in which a sower cast his seeds on the roadside, on rocky ground, among thorns, and onto good soil. Only the seeds thrown on good soil sprout and bear fruit. The sower is Jesus and the seeds are his words, which only bear fruit when they take root in the heart of the faithful, where they "will conquer lusts and cleanse the heart from sins."

This famous biblical parable is also found in the Arabic *Bilawhar and Būdhāsaf*. It is most likely then that it comes into our tale from an Arabic source, rather than directly from the New Testament, further evidence of the circulation of biblical texts among Islamic scholars.[4]

Iodasaph says, "I place my hope in Christ, that whatever

seed you implant in me may sprout up and bring forth much fruit. Now convey to me the likeness of the transitory world, and how it deludes those who cherish it." Balahvar replies with the parable of the man who falls into an abyss (known elsewhere as the parable of the man in the well). This is the one parable in the story that is clearly of Indian origin; it is found in Indian and Buddhist texts, including the *Mahābhārata*. It was included in *Kalīlah and Dimnah*, a widely circulating Arabic translation of the Indian *Pañcatantra* from 750 CE, and the Arabic *Bilawhar and Būdhāsaf* probably borrows it from this source.[5] Balahvar begins the story: "This transitory life and all that cherish it resemble a man pursued by a raging elephant, which cornered him inside a fearsome abyss." He then recounts that when the man leapt into the pit to escape the elephant, he grabbed two tree branches that grew over the opening, thus saving himself from falling into its depths. He was also able to find a place below him to support his feet. Now safe from the raging elephant, at least for the time being, he took a moment to assess his situation. Looking up, he saw that two mice, one black and one white, were gnawing away at the roots of the tree whose branches supported him. Looking down into the abyss, he realized that he had leapt into a dragon's lair and that the dragon was at the bottom with open jaws, awaiting his fall. Closer by, he looked down at his feet and saw four adders emerging from the side of the cliff where he stood. Looking up again, he saw that some honey was dripping down from the branches of the tree. He opened his mouth and it fell onto his tongue. Savoring its sweetness, he forgot his peril.

Balahvar explained to the prince that the elephant represents death, constantly pursuing man. The abyss is the world. The two branches represent a person's lifespan, slowly being severed by the passage of day and night, represented by the white and black mice. The four snakes were the four elements of earth, water, fire, and air that constitute the body; if one is damaged, life comes to an end. The dragon represents hell into which lovers of the world must eventually fall. Rather than recognizing their plight, they savor the sweet honey, which is like the fleeting pleasures of the world.

In the course of his conversation with the prince, Balahvar reveals that he belongs to a community of Christian hermits who have been driven out of India by King Abenes. They do not care for the king or his rule, he explains, because they serve a greater lord: Jesus Christ. When the prince asks him how old he is, Balahvar replies that he is twelve years old. Iodasaph is puzzled, and the hermit explains that although he was born sixty years earlier, a man is dead until he places his faith in Christ, and he has been a Christian for only twelve years.

Balahvar teaches the prince with his parables, using them to describe the virtues of the ascetic life and to explain Christian doctrine and belief. His discourses after each parable vary in length; one of the more substantial is an exhortation to make proper use of reason to arrive at the truth and to resist the devil's claims that there is no profit in learning: "A sage should not lose heart at his failure to gain admission through one door of knowledge, but should then proceed to make trial of a second. Nor should ignorance of one aspect of a matter cause a man to abandon the subject altogether. No man can attain knowledge of everything he seeks; nor is all knowledge necessarily profitable, nor all ignorance invariably harmful." The hermit goes on to provide arguments for the existence of God and the truth of the resurrection, and explains how to recognize a false prophet.

## *Balahvar Is Discovered*

As in the Arabic story, the prince's retainers take notice of Balahvar's frequent and extended audiences at the palace. Zadan, one of the prince's servants, suspects that the visitor may be a Christian. His loyalty is divided between the prince and the king, but he fears the king's punishment more than he values the prince's friendship. He tells Iodasaph that he will inform the king of the hermit's visits if Iodasaph continues to receive him. If the prince does not wish him to speak to the king, he explains, he will have to dismiss Balahvar. Iodasaph suggests that before deciding what to do, Zadan should hide behind a curtain and listen to what Balahvar says when he next comes to speak to the prince. Zadan agrees. He hears the monk's words, praises Balahvar's description of the vanity of the world, and explains that such teachings have long been absent from King Abenes's kingdom: "since the time when the king persecuted and banned the Christian faith, we have no more been allowed to hear such tidings, for fear that our hearts might receive and cherish this doctrine." Zadan will not convert because of his loyalty to the king, he tells the prince; however, Iodasaph should do so if he is willing to bear his father's wrath.

Once the prince accepts the Christian faith, Balahvar prepares to depart. The prince begs to accompany him, but the hermit refuses, saying that the king will claim his son has been abducted and use the claim as a pretext to hunt down the Christians and destroy them. The prince offers gifts to his teacher, but Balahvar again declines. He has no use for jewels or rich clothing, he explains. When the prince asks Balahvar to remove his merchant's robes and reveal how he looks when he is living with his fellow monks, Balahvar takes off his robes, "exposing his entire skin drawn over his bones like the hide of a man dead through excessive fasting, stretched tightly over thin canes." He wears only a tattered apron made of hair, which he eventually gives to Iodasaph in exchange for an equally worn garment. Balahvar then gives the prince detailed instructions on how to live: "Do not flatter yourself, or trust others except those who merit confidence. Distrust and analyze your own impulses, and cast out your lustful desires. Spend the days of your life in such a way that you may be found each day in perfect obedience to God and Our Saviour Jesus Christ, and be prepared to encounter death at any moment." After embracing the prince tearfully, Balahvar departs.

As Book III begins, Zadan feigns illness in order to be relieved of serving the prince. Summoned by the king, Zadan tells the king about the visits of Balahvar and the prince's conversion. Although angry and dismayed, the king hides his feelings and seeks a way to win back his son. As in the Arabic version, the king sends for his councilor Rakhis, who presents the plan to capture the Christian hermit and bring him to the city to debate the pagan philosophers; the Christians will be defeated and the prince will then return to his senses. However, the Georgian *Balavariani* eliminates Rakhis's magical transformation into the likeness of the hermit and introduces a new character into the episode: Nakhor is a man who looks just like Balahvar and will take his place if the hermit cannot be found. According to the plan devised by Rakhis and the king, Nakhor will lose the debate intentionally, and the prince, thinking his master has been bested, will abandon his beliefs.

While seeking Balahvar, Rakhis and his soldiers encounter a group of Christian monks whose leader carries bones hanging from a cord. When they will not tell Rakhis where Balahvar can be found, he takes them to the king, who threatens them with death. As in the Arabic version, the king's threats do not move the monks; they yearn to join those whose relics they carry. The monks ask the king why he persecutes Christians. He replies, "This wrath of mine serves as a lesson both for them and for the nation, so that the land may not become waste, and also to punish those ascetics for having no love for the good things of earth." The leader of the ascetics disputes the king's claim, arguing that the king wishes them to return to the world only to exploit them: "The only things you allow your subjects to enjoy are those which you can readily spare. It is clear you seek your own advantage and not your neighbor's, and this is why you want us to revert to the world." Enraged by the Christians' lack of fear, the king commands their hands and feet to be cut off and their eyes gouged out and cast onto the road. His men carry out the king's orders, leaving the ascetics dead.

The king's men do not find Balahvar, and Nakhor takes his place, pretending to be the captured hermit. When the prince hears that Balahvar has been imprisoned by the king he despairs, but Barakhia, one of the king's courtiers and a secret Christian, learns of the plot and informs the prince about the substitution.

Before resorting to Rakhis's plan for the staged disputation, King Abenes confronts Iodasaph about his conversion. In a long and heated argument, the king tells the prince how disappointed he is by his son's betrayal: "You have abandoned my faith, opposed my wishes through your willfulness, cast doubt on the religion of your ancestors, and delivered your downy curls into the hands of false men and seducers, who will lead you into sorrow and hurl you into perdition." Iodasaph replies that he had wished to keep his faith secret from his father: "My desire is to conform outwardly in all respects to the pattern which you fondly cherished for me, so that when I die, your heart may not overflow with bitterness because of me." Iodasaph hid his faith to show his filial devotion, he explains; he did not invite his father to join his faith because he thought him too addicted to his sinful ways ever to leave them. Although his secret may cause his father grief now, the prince declares that it will bring him great joy in the future and promises that he will continue to maintain appearances and not make their differences public. In return, he asks that his father not expect him to return to idolatry and that he be left in peace to practice privately.

The king responds by cursing his son, lamenting his ingratitude for all the good things he has given him over the course of the prince's life. If Iodasaph were to actually live the ascetic life that he praises so ardently, he would soon come to his senses and return to the palace, the king claims. Abenes blames himself for his son's decision; if he had exposed his son to life's bitterness from the beginning, he would better appreciate the sweet things of life. The prince protests that his father speaks to him as if he were a child. He concedes that the life his father has chosen for him is beautiful, yet it is also transient. If his father could guarantee that its beauty would not pass away, then it would be truly good. "But since you cannot guarantee this, why should you not forgive me if I choose to renounce it, thereby to attain the life which is most to be desired? Why are you astonished, O king, at my yearning for eternal blessings, rather than being amazed at your own attachment to the transitory pleasures of the world?" By driving the Christians into the wilderness, Iodasaph claims, the king has cast his son into a spiritual wilderness without a guide and surrounded him with devils. Iodasaph's despair in this world only increases his longing for the next. Fearing that he may truly lose his temper, the king rises and leaves.

But the king returns the next day and embraces his son, embarking on a long defense of himself as a just and generous king and reminding Iodasaph of his generosity as a patron of the priests and their temples, and of his charity to widows, orphans, and cripples. How then can Iodasaph accuse him of being capricious and self-indulgent, and of following a path to perdition? Perhaps the prince has been possessed by a devil who causes him to believe in these falsehoods. But the prince is unmoved, telling his father that like all mortals, he will die soon and will have to give an account of his words and deeds. Only the servants of Christ understand the true path.

The king and his son find no common ground in their dispute. Although the king claims to act virtuously, he does not describe his acts as conforming to the teaching of a prophet as in the Arabic text, and indeed, the long discussion between the prince and the king about al-Budd and his teachings is entirely absent from the *Balavariani*. It may have been missing from the Arabic version used by the Georgian adaptors, or it may have been excised because the appeal to the teachings of al-Budd makes little sense in the Christian context of the *Balavariani*. Whatever the reason for its absence, the elimination of the dispute between father and son about who is the more faithful follower of al-Budd also eliminates any common purpose and intensifies the conflict between the two.

And yet despite his anger and resentment, the king is almost convinced to renounce the pleasures of the world when he hears Iodasaph's eloquent defense of his faith. An inner voice forestalls his conversion, however: "You cannot exist a single day without the things you are used to, and if you admit your error and change your convictions, you will incur bitterness and reproach." Abenes then suggests to his son that a debate be held between a Christian hermit and a pagan priest. Iodasaph agrees, and the king declares an amnesty so that all Christians may attend.

On the day of the debate, the king sits on his throne and Iodasaph sits on the ground. No Christians dare to attend except for the courtier Barakhia, who had earlier alerted the prince to the substitution of Nakhor for his teacher. The debate between the Christian and the pagans is much like the debate between the people of the Religion and the idolaters in the Arabic story. The king and Iodasaph threaten their respective representatives with death if they are not victorious. Realizing that his life is at stake, Nakhor, impersonating Balahvar, condemns idolatry and extols Christianity with an eloquence that the true Balahvar could not have equaled. The king is angry that Nakhor has deviated from the agreed-upon plan and he himself begins to dispute with the disguised hermit. Fearing the king's wrath, Nakhor falters, but Iodasaph intercedes, suggesting that the king either turn Nakhor over to him and allow them to depart in peace, or that the idolater priests depart with Iodasaph and Nakhor should accompany the king. The king fears that his son will convert his own priests to Christianity and he allows Nakhor to depart, still hoping that the hermit might somehow shake his son's faith. When Iodasaph and Nakhor are alone, the prince tells the disguised Nakhor that he knows his true identity and urges him to embrace in his heart the faith he had professed with his lips. Nakhor agrees immediately and, with the prince's permission, departs for the wilderness to join the Christian hermits.

## The King Doubts His Idols

At the news of Nakhor's conversion the king's faith in his idols wavers further. The priests fear they are losing the support of their monarch and they summon a respected pagan hermit named Thedma to revive the king's commitment to their religion. Thedma claims that if the king will command sacrifices to the idols he will help him win back his son. King Abenes is reluctant. He tells the hermit that he will celebrate an upcoming religious festival only if Thedma can convince him of the truth of idolatry. Unlike later versions, in the Georgian redaction the king uses a parable to defend his need to know that his personal gods are true deities.

King Abenes relates the story of a military commander who knew "the fickleness and weakness of womankind" and feared that his beautiful wife would be unfaithful to him. He told his wife that his enemy would try to seduce her, and she should guard herself closely. When she experienced sexual desire she should signal her husband by letting her hair down. When he saw the sign, he would come to her and satisfy her desires, and his enemy would not win his wife. The woman did as her husband asked and they lived together in harmony. One day an enemy approached the city and the warrior husband prepared for battle. The wife saw her husband looking splendid in his armor and she was filled with desire. She let down her hair and her husband went back into his house to satisfy his wife's passion. By the time he ventured out to fight, the enemy had been defeated and the army was returning from the battle. The other soldiers mocked him, saying that he had been too frightened to fight. The commander responded, "My private foe was battling with me! I could not leave him in order to fight outside enemies, for he was my most domestic and immediate foe. Now that I have conquered him, I can rejoin your company."

King Abenes uses the story to describe his own need to verify that his gods are true deities: "Thus it is with us, O Thedma!," he says to the hermit who has come to admonish him for not preparing sacrifices to his gods. "Today we are involved in an affair which affects both us and the idols. But first of all I have to exterminate my own personal enemies. If afterwards we establish that the gods are really gods, then we shall offer up sacrifices to them. But if they cannot be proved genuine deities, what can such imaginary beings profit us?" It is perhaps no coincidence that King Abenes uses a story about sexual fidelity to describe loyalty to his gods; the sexual pleasure described in the parable suggests the king's own attachments to the physical pleasures of the world, attachments that his son has rejected and that the king will shortly try to revive when he sends young women to try to seduce Iodasaph and draw him away from his Christian faith. The parable also introduces explicitly misogynistic sentiments into the story—"I know the fickleness and weakness of womankind," says the warrior husband—and identifies women's infidelity as a danger to men, much as the king's attempt to have young women seduce his son casts women as a danger for the man who would renounce the world.

The king's wavering faith in his gods is an element that receives less emphasis as the story is transmitted and further translated. In subsequent versions, the contrast between good and evil is starker, the opposition between the idolatrous king and his Christian son more polarized. Although the king begins to suspect the truth of Christianity and neglects his gods in his disappointment at their failure to retain his son's faith, he holds to his religion because he will not give up his realm, his rank, or his privileges. But no other Christian version of the story includes the king's parable about the warrior and his wife, and other versions do not recount the king's questioning of his idols in such explicit terms.

When the king reveals his doubts, Thedma reacts with

anger and Abenes understands that the pagan hermit cannot confirm his faith. The king's doubts increase and he moves closer to converting to Christianity, but again his will to convert is impeded by his love for the pleasures of the world. He acquiesces to Thedma's demand that he organize a great celebration of the idols, and the hermit advises the king on how to shake his son's Christian beliefs. At the suggestion of Thedma (who tells him the parable of the boy who had never seen women), Abenes sends beautiful women to seduce his son. Iodasaph falls in love with the most beautiful and intelligent among them, a slave princess. She bargains with him, offering conversion for sex, and Iodasaph agrees, "because his natural instincts inclined him to do so." But before they are united, Jesus intervenes, and during a night of prayer the prince falls asleep and dreams of the glories of heaven that are the reward for the saints and the steadfast. In his dream, he sees the women who tempted him. They now appear "more hideous and unsightly than dogs' or pigs' snouts." He then has a vision of hell and sees the punishment reserved for those who fall in love with the world. When the prince awakes, the women are all weeping because they think he has died. Iodasaph's desire for them has been changed by his vision; as in his dream, their beauty cannot compare to the glories he saw in heaven. The women are insignificant and ugly to him, and he no longer desires them.

The account of the prince's vision follows the story found in *Bilawhar and Būdhāsaf*, but in the Georgian version, Iodasaph remains chaste. Although he initially agrees to the beautiful princess's bargain of sex in exchange for conversion, divine intervention prevents him from enacting the exchange. The Georgian version of the story emphasizes virginity in addition to chastity and reflects the growing importance of virginity in the medieval Christian idea of bodily purity. It also disrupts the genealogical succession maintained in the earlier versions of the story. The Christian story valorizes virginity over lineage, whereas in *Bilawhar and Būdhāsaf*, as in the life of the Buddha, the pious prince engenders a son before withdrawing from the world.

In the *Balavariani*, the king learns of his son's vision and comes to see him. Iodasaph asks his permission to go into the wilderness. The king is again cast into despair, fearing that one of his enemies will kidnap or kill the prince. The Georgian story describes King Abenes's resistance to asceticism in both religious and political terms. But whereas in *Bilawhar and Būdhāsaf* the king's concern for the future of his kingdom focuses on his grandson, the Georgian version emphasizes the king's effort to persuade his own son to take his throne. Abenes proposes to divide his kingdom in two and give half to Iodasaph, hoping that the responsibilities of kingship will bind his son to the world. The prince understands his father's intent, and so refuses. He knows nothing of the world and is unfit to rule, the prince claims, and asks again for his father's permission to join the Christians in the wilderness. Another long argument between father and son follows, and the prince finally agrees to take half the kingdom when the king allows him to openly preach the Gospel in his own land. The king divides his lands, treasury, and armory in two. He allows anyone who so wishes to accompany the prince to his new kingdom and agrees to the prince's request that all those in prison be released into his care.

Iodasaph is a just and generous king. He lives modestly and sells his royal possessions to feed the poor. Multitudes are baptized each day and Christians who had long hidden their faith flock to his kingdom. Iodasaph soon rules over more people than his father. Meanwhile, as King Abenes's power wanes, his own people begin to turn against him, and the king fears assassination. His councilors advise him to abdicate and allow Iodasaph to rule the reunited kingdom, but the king resists. His councilors hold to their advice even though they fear that, in a reunited kingdom, they themselves may be punished along with the king for their past persecution of the Christians. Abenes finally writes to Iodasaph, proposing reunification on the condition that the idolaters be allowed to practice their religion. Iodasaph refuses that condition but offers to discuss the unification of their lands with a delegation of elders from his father's kingdom. A colloquy of wise pagans and Christian monks is convened, at the end of which the idolaters ask Iodasaph whether they would be punished under his rule. He answers that all who convert will be forgiven. As a result the king and all of his people (with the exception of Thedma) tell Iodasaph of their wish to convert to Christianity. Iodasaph welcomes them on the condition that they destroy their idols and their temples, which they do. Eventually, Thedma comes to the court of Iodasaph and engages him in a long debate about idolatry and Christianity, at the conclusion of which he too is converted. He devotes all his efforts to living a pious life and he publicly atones for his past crimes. On his deathbed King

Abenes fears the punishment that awaits him for all his sins, but his son assures him that God is a merciful judge. The king dies in peace praising God. His son buries him and remains at his tomb in prayer for seven days. On the eighth day he announces his intention to renounce the throne and go into the wilderness, but the people tearfully implore him to remain.

The reluctance of Iodasaph's people to allow him to depart echoes the account of the prince's departure in *Bilawhar and Būdhāsaf*, but it omits the section of the Arabic story that is clearly inspired by the life of the Buddha: the prince's discovery of the sacred tree after his departure from the palace, his ascent into heaven, and his return to teach the world and convert his father before his death. In the Georgian version, the conversion of the father is retained, but after the king's death, the prince leaves his kingdom to seek his teacher.

## Bodies and Bones

King Iodasaph departs from his palace under the cover of night, leaving behind a charter designating Barakhia as his successor, but his subjects follow him. They find him praying in a valley and beg him to return. He reluctantly accompanies them back to his palace, but again announces his decision to abandon his reign. Iodasaph places the royal signet ring on Barakhia's finger and delivers a long speech on how Barakhia should rule as a pious king. "Subject every problem to careful trial, just as I was tried out by Balahvar. He gave me no guidance on earthly matters, but through the medium of spiritual guidance enabled me to manage even earthly affairs through God's grace." Iodasaph then dons the hair apron he had received from Balahvar and sets out for Sarandib in search of his teacher. He finds him two years later and they rejoice at their reunion. In the *Balavariani*, Iodasaph has only a few days with his teacher before Balahvar's death draws near. Iodasaph wails in despair, "O father Balahvar, you have not given full effect of your love towards me! For you are departing to enjoy repose from the woes of this world, and leaving me all alone in great grief in a strange land." Balahvar comforts him, telling Iodasaph that they will meet again soon. Iodasaph buries his teacher in a grotto and then falls asleep and dreams that men approach him bearing crowns. One man carries two crowns that shine more brightly than the others. The man tells him that one is for him and one for his father. Iodasaph is resentful and protests that he has done so much for his faith, while his father merely repented, and only at the very end of his life—why should they receive equal rewards? Balahvar appears to him and reminds the prince that he should rejoice in his father's salvation and in the reward that will come to them both. Iodasaph accepts his teacher's lesson and prays for forgiveness.

Long after his own conversion and establishment of a Christian kingdom, Iodasaph appears to struggle with jealousy. Here, again, he is very different from the Buddha, who never suffered a moment of weakness over the course of his life. It is said that he occasionally felt physical pain, the consequences of deeds done in lives long past. For example, he sometimes had back pain because in a previous life as a wrestler he had broken his opponent's back. But the Buddha was free from all forms of mental anguish and pain. Few of even the greatest of Christian saints achieved such equanimity. We recall that the aged Saint Jerome is often depicted with a large stone at hand, ready to beat his bare and bony breast when tortured by temptation. It appears that for Buddhist saints, purity is achieved with the attainment of enlightenment, while in Christianity, purity awaits in heaven.

Some time after the death of his master, Iodasaph dies. A hermit who lives nearby comes to lay his body in the cave next to Balahvar's. King Barakhia and a great multitude come and retrieve the bodies. They bring them back to Iodasaph's former kingdom and enshrine them in one of the churches he built there. Many come to pray before their relics and are cured of illness and infirmity.

As we noted in Chapter Two, the account of the prince's death in *Bilawhar and Būdhāsaf* echoes accounts of the Buddha's death. Būdhāsaf's companion makes a smooth place for him on the ground; he lies down with his face toward the east and dies. After briefly noting that his descendants rule the land according to his religion, the story ends. There is no mention of Būdhāsaf's burial and there is no indication that his body is venerated. The Georgian adaptor brings the protagonist fully into Christian theology by giving him and his teacher saintly qualities: their bodies are miracle-working relics.

The miraculous qualities of bodies are also at stake in the Arabic story, but in a more distant way. In *Bilawhar and Būdhāsaf*, a holy corpse is described as having the power to change the living in the story of the 'Anqā's chicks. They consume al-Budd's corpse and because of his virtuous life, the young birds are filled with piety, goodness, sincerity, knowledge, and wisdom. The bodies of Balahvar and Iodasaph are similarly effective in that they intervene in the world of the living. They testify to the saintly qualities of the prince and his teacher, and later versions of the story will describe the uncorrupted nature of the bodies that King Barakhia and his people find when they retrieve their bodies from the desert. The Christian versions of the story of the prince and his master stress the miracle-working powers of the two holy men's bodies.

> The king arose with a great multitude and came to that place together with his princes and bore away the bodies of both the saints, and enclosed them within urns adorned with gold. And Barakhia laid these relics within a hallowed church dedicated to the worship of the Holy Trinity, and exalted them with every mark of honour. Many who were rendered infirm by grievous ailments were delivered from them by these relics, which constantly wrought miracles. And the king and all the people saw this and glorified Christ our God, who readily grants success in all things to those who love him; for to Him belong glory and honour, grace and adoration together with the Father who has no beginning and the Holy Spirit, giver of life, now and always and for all eternity, Amen.

Through the miracles their bodies accomplish, Balahvar and Iodasaph continue to serve their God, no longer in the desert but in the world they left, ironically enshrined in gold vessels like those they renounced in life.

At the time the anonymous Georgian authors turned the Arabic *Bilawhar and Būdhāsaf* into *Balahvar and Iodasaph*, Marwan the Deaf had conquered Iberia and had put to death the pious Christian princes Davit and Constantine Mkheidze after they eloquently defended their faith. We would not wish to read the *Balavariani* as a simple roman à clef. Still, the story of the pious Georgian princes provides a possible answer to how a Muslim ascetic became a Christian saint: it is not, or not only, the sanctity of the son that motivates the adaptation of the story to a Christian context. It is also the cruel and vengeful nature of the father, who rules so ruthlessly over his realm.

In the Christian retelling, the idolatrous king becomes a persecutor of Christians, who are forced to either hide their faith or die. The evil king does so not simply because he hates Christianity but because he fears that the Christians will revolt against him and he will lose his throne. The king himself is an idolater, a polemical term that was used in the Middle Ages to name anyone who practiced an alien religion, which often simply meant a religion other than Christianity. The Georgian Christians may be covertly protesting against the brutal regime of Marwan the Deaf and giving their country's plight a happy ending: the evil king is converted and the pious prince restores the Christian faith. The *Balavariani* acts as a revenge fantasy, with the Georgian monks creating characters who overthrow and convert the idolaters in the tale.

During the same period, the Buddhists of India (whom, as we shall see, Europeans would come to call idolaters) were writing their own revenge fantasy. In the wake of devastating Muslim raids on Buddhist monasteries in northern India, in the eleventh century a text appeared called the *Kālacakra*

*Tantra*, a text traditionally attributed to the Buddha (although it was composed more than a millennium after his death). It describes a kingdom hidden deep in the Himalayas that is a special domain for the practice of Buddhism and is protected by a great king. The kingdom is called Shambhala (the likely inspiration for James Hilton's Shangri-La). At some point in the future, a great Buddhist army will sweep out of the Himalayas and defeat the barbarians in an apocalyptic battle. Who are the barbarians? They are said to come from the land of Makha. They cut off the ends of their penises (i.e., practice circumcision), eat camel meat, and follow the teachings of one Madhumati, a Sanskrit term meaning "mind of mead," or, less politely, "wino." The *Kālacakra Tantra* would become one of the most influential texts of the last days of Indian Buddhism.

The Georgian tale composed in Jerusalem could have served a similar purpose: looking to a future free of persecution, with the idolaters converted. Iodasaph was quickly accepted as a saint in Georgia. A lengthy hymn of exaltation was composed to him, likely in the ninth or tenth century, not long after *Bilawhar and Būdhāsaf* is thought to have been translated into Georgian and a time when Georgia was still under Muslim rule. The hymn is preserved in a manuscript from 1065 and celebrates the reward God has given Iodasaph for following the narrow path to salvation. The song addresses the saint: "He set upon you the imperishable crown, and assigned you a place among the immortal souls," and then continues:

> Your illustrious festival delights with joy divine the hearts of those who intone their hymn to you with faith; they sound a new trumpet, and with the harp of the spirit as

with the psaltery they chant in unison with the sweet voice of the triumphal organ.

You destroyed the error of polytheism, O God-clad one, and proclaimed the divine unity of the Holy Trinity, and the Word born of the Father before all ages, equal with Him in divine power, the offspring of a virgin's womb.

Now boldly beseech God before whose presence you stand, O righteous one, to preserve the churches inviolate, and grant the nation of true believers and their orthodox sovereign victory over the infidel foe, for the exaltation of Christendom.

By the power of your prayers, O worthy one, you drove out of your country the foul devils and all their host, overturned the filthy tabernacles of the idols, and entirely dispelled their reeking fumes which darkened the atmosphere, O blessed one; and you tore away the veil of obscurity from the eyes of men's reason.

Your arms dealt mortal wounds to that wicked deceiver when you raised up the wood of the life-giving Cross and put on the invincible armour of its might; and you shattered his fangs and dragged from his poisonous jaws countless souls and presented them victorious before God.[6]

In the *Balavariani*, the "people of the Religion" described in *Bilawhar and Būdhāsaf* have become Christian ascetics, and debates about the Religion have become lessons in Christian doctrine that are interspersed throughout the Georgian story: in Balahvar's lessons to the prince, in the confrontations between the king and his son, in the debate between Nakhor and the pagan philosophers, in the passages that recount Iodasaph's decision to accept half of his father's kingdom, and even in the attempted seduction scene. Balahvar uses parables to teach Iodasaph and his teachings are largely a series of parables, as in the Arabic *Bilawhar and Būdhāsaf*, but here they illustrate Christian truths. A number of the parables have been eliminated in the Georgian text—whereas the Arabic *Bilawhar and Būdhāsaf* includes twenty-nine, the *Balavariani* has fifteen—and the parables used to illustrate the virtues of ascetic practice in the Arabic text now illustrate the values of Christian ascetic practice.

Iodasaph drove the idolaters from India, or in the words of the hymn, "released the race of Indians by God's power from their benighted devil-worship." In medieval Georgia, he became a saint and was called upon to intercede at the throne of God to preserve the Christian church of Georgia and to grant the nation of the faithful and their pious king victory over the infidel. Aided by the saint, the Christians could do as Iodasaph had done and drive the "foul devils" and their host from Georgia. Tenth-century Georgians living under Muslim rule found their savior in an Arabic text. But in order for Iodasaph to be more than a local hero, his story would need to be told in yet another language.

# CHAPTER FOUR

# The Saint Is Translated:
# Greek and Latin Versions of
# the *Barlaam* Legend

The Georgian authors of the *Balavariani* took much of the story directly from its Arabic version, but they never identified their text as a translation. It was almost a millennium later scholars demonstrated that the *Balavariani* came from the Arabic *Bilawhar and Būdhāsaf.* The Georgian silence is not unusual. Medieval authors borrowed freely from one another and from preexisting texts. They translated or copied their sources, elaborating and adapting them to their own uses. If they identified those sources, it was to demonstrate the authority of their texts, rather than to suggest that they were derivative or somehow secondary.

Just as the tenth-century Georgian *Balavariani* was silent about its Arabic origins, so too the eleventh-century Greek *Barlaam and Ioasaph* was silent about its Georgian source. In fact, the Greek text describes a more direct origin for the narrative it recounts. In the prologue, the author alludes to the biblical story of the man who hid away the talents given to him by his lord and states that he will not make the same mistake: "Heedful of the danger hanging over that servant who, having received the talent from his lord, buried it in the earth, and hid that which was given him to trade, I will in no way pass over in silence the edifying story that has come to me, delivered by devout men from the inner land of the Ethiopians, whom our tale calls Indians, and translated from trustworthy records."[1] The conflation of India and Ethiopia has a long history, particularly in literary texts, and the identity of the Indians mentioned in the Greek *Barlaam and Ioasaph* would be a subject of much speculation in the nineteenth century.[2] During the earlier centuries they were assumed to be Christians from India.

## Saint Thomas in India

In many medieval Western texts, "Ethiopia" is a vaguely defined region somewhere east of Europe. It has little geographical specificity and often indicates a faraway land where monstrous races dwell.[3] But in *Barlaam and Ioasaph* Ethiopia is identified with India and located with some specificity: "The country of the Indians, as it is called, is vast and populous, lying far beyond Egypt. On the side of Egypt it is washed by seas and navigable gulfs, but on the mainland it borders Persia, a land formerly darkened with the gloom of idolatry, barbarous to the last degree, and wholly given up to unlawful practices." The narrator explains that the Indians have been saved from idolatry by Christianity, brought to their land by the apostle Thomas himself.

As described in the New Testament's Acts of the Apostles, after the resurrection of Jesus the Holy Spirit appeared in the form of flames above the heads of the apostles and gave them the gift of tongues so that they could go throughout the world to preach the Gospel. *Barlaam and Ioasaph* describes the scene: "[God] sent down the Comforter, the Holy Ghost, to his eye-witnesses and disciples, in the shape of fiery tongues, and dispatched them unto all nations, to give light to those who dwelled in the darkness of ignorance, and to baptize them in the Name of the Father, and of the Son, and of the Holy Ghost. It fell to some of the Apostles to travel to the far-off East and to some to journey to the West, while others traversed the regions North and South, fulfilling their appointed tasks, then it was, I say, that one of the company of Christ's Twelve Apostles, most holy Thomas, was sent out to the land of the Indians, preaching the Gospel of Salvation."

According to legend, although not in the Gospels, when the disciples drew lots to decide where they would take their mission, India fell to Thomas—the same Thomas known as "Doubting Thomas" because of his initial failure to believe in Jesus's resurrection. Thomas objected to his lot, saying, "I am a Hebrew man. How can I go amongst the Indians and preach the truth?" But he would have no choice. Not long after, Jesus appeared in the marketplace and sold Thomas to an Indian king. Traveling against his will, Thomas is said to have converted kings in both northern and southern India before being martyred by a pagan king. Through his preaching, in India "the darkness of superstition was banished, and men were delivered from idolatrous sacrifices and abominations, and added to the true Faith, and being thus transformed by the hands of the Apostle, were made members of Christ's household by baptism, and, waxing ever with fresh increase, advanced in the blameless Faith and built churches in all their lands," in the words of the Greek narrator.

The oldest source for Saint Thomas's life is the apocryphal *Acts of Saint Thomas*, originally written in Syriac and probably composed between the middle of the third century and the end of the fourth in Edessa, the site of one of two shrines to Thomas. Marco Polo speaks of a visit to Saint Thomas's tomb in India. The shrine's red earth was considered to have miraculous healing properties, he notes, and both Muslims and Christians venerated the site. When the Portuguese arrived at the end of the fifteenth century, they believed that the Christians they found in southern India were the descendants of Thomas's converts.

The narrator of *Barlaam and Ioasaph* situates his story in the wake of Thomas's mission to India. At the time of the Desert Fathers, he tells us, "when monasteries began to be formed in Egypt, and numbers of monks banded themselves together, and when the fame of their virtues and Angelic conversation had gone out into all the ends of the world and came to the Indians, it stirred them up also to the same zeal, and many of them forsook everything and withdrew to the deserts; and, though but men in mortal bodies, they adopted the spiritual life of Angels." All of this is an innovation of the Greek text, which provides something of a creation myth for the story of the pious prince and his idolatrous father: the story was brought west from India, carried on a long and dangerous journey by devout Christians who wanted the story to be known to the Christian world. They delivered it to the narrator, presumably a monk, who would transcribe the story. The prologue thus locates *Barlaam and Ioasaph* within the sacred history of the church, placing it in an unbroken historical circuit, beginning with the Pentecost, which inspired the mission of the apostle Thomas to India. The prologue next invokes the Desert Fathers of the Egyptian wilderness, whose sanctity, according to the story, inspired a similar ascetic movement in India. The Christian monks of India were persecuted by the idolatrous King Abenner, but, after his conversion by Barlaam, Ioasaph restored India to the Christian faith. To complete the circuit, pious men carried the good tidings from faraway India to the Holy Land, where Saint Thomas had embarked on his mission so long ago. To proclaim Ioasaph's triumph to the elders of the church, the story brought from India had now been rendered into Greek.

Greek was the language of the church, the language of the letters of the apostle Paul, and the language of the Church Fathers. The narrator of *Barlaam and Ioasaph* does not say that he translated the story, only that he recorded it, but he draws attention to his role in the story's transmission in the brief epilogue that begins, "Here ends this history, which I have written, to the best of my ability, just as I heard it from the truthful lips of the worthy men who delivered it unto me." He does not say which language the "Indians" had spoken to him. The anonymous author represents himself as a scribe who records the words of the pilgrims. The eyewitness presence he claims for the transmission would add authority to the text.

## Saint John of Damascus

Until the late nineteenth century, the Greek text of *Barlaam and Ioasaph* was believed to be the original version of the story, in part because of the narrator's claim to have composed it from an oral account and in part because no prior versions had been identified. Its author was thought to be Saint John of Damascus (ca. 676–749 CE), and for a long time this attribution was not questioned. (A rare instance of doubt about the authorship seems to have been raised in an early eighteenth-century edition of John of Damascus's works where *Barlaam and Ioasaph* is relegated to an appendix, suggesting that the compiler questioned its authenticity as one of John's works.)

There were several reasons for the enduring attribution. The Greek story survives in two dozen manuscripts, the oldest dating from the eleventh century, and some identify the author as "John, monk of the monastery of St. Sabas." Since a tenth-century narrative of the life of John of Damascus recounts that he left the secular world to become a priest at the monastery of St. Sabas, located near Jerusalem, the famous John of Damascus was taken to be the author of *Barlaam and Ioasaph*. The attribution was also suggested by quotations from John of Damascus's writings in *Barlaam and Ioasaph*. It must have seemed logical to assume that the text had been authored by this well-known figure.

According to hagiographical accounts, John was born in Damascus, capital of the Muslim Umayyad caliphate. He was the son of a devout Christian who served at the court of the caliph, and, after his father's death, John was made chief councilor of Damascus. It was there that he wrote famous defenses of the veneration of icons, condemning the ban on their worship by the Byzantine emperor Leo III the Isaurian in Constantinople. The simple style of his three letters in defense of iconology generated much support. However, Christian iconoclasts, who wished to eliminate icons from Christian worship, plotted to destroy John and his influence. They forged a letter from him to Christians in Constantinople in which he offered to aid them in the conquest of Muslim Damascus. The letter was shown to the caliph, who was deceived by the forgery and commanded that the offending hand that wrote the letter be cut off and displayed in public. John's hand was severed, but then miraculously restored by the Virgin Mary. It was after these events that John is said to have left his position in Damascus to enter the monastery of St. Sabas, where he was ordained as a priest and lived for the rest of his life.

This traditional account of John's prominent role at the Muslim court is now disputed. John's father is mentioned in Muslim sources but John himself does not appear, and it is more likely that his three letters in support of the veneration of images were written when he was at St. Sabas and not while he was in Damascus. But as the son of a Syrian Christian who served at the Muslim court, John is likely to have had some association with Muslims, and he was condemned by his enemies as a "cursed favorer of Saracens [Muslims]," a "traitorous worshipper of images," a "wronger of Jesus Christ," and a "bad interpreter of the Scriptures." Ultimately, though, the iconoclasts lost the battle over the place of icons in the rituals of what would become the Eastern Orthodox Church, and in 787

CE John's good name was posthumously restored at a church council in Nicea. The tenth-century hagiographical account of his life contributes to his status as a Father of the Church and a saint, although it was only in the nineteenth century that John of Damascus was inserted into the General Roman Calendar of saints.

Although the position of John of Damascus carried the day in the iconoclasm controversy, the question of the status of images in Christian devotion would continue to surface in the medieval church, and a sharp distinction would later be drawn between the worship of icons and the worship of idols (the question was considered at length by Thomas Aquinas). Thus, for medieval readers of *Barlaam and Ioasaph*, it would not have seemed strange that the saint most closely associated with the defense of icons would compose a text that condemned idols. John even appears as a character in at least one translation of the story; in his thirteenth-century Old French *Barlaam et Josaphat*, Gui de Cambrai represents John as an archbishop who joins Josaphat in his Christian kingdom, where he converts the pagans from idolatry. Gui's use of the figure of the archbishop, as he calls him, suggests the prestige associated with John of Damascus in the Middle Ages, and his purported authorship of *Barlaam and Josaphat* surely contributed to the popularity of the story.

Many medieval texts circulated in compilations: a collection of saints' lives, for example, or a group of religious texts, or, in some cases, a seemingly random collection of texts that might include edifying tales, sermons, stories, or poetry. Manuscripts did not usually include a separate title page identifying the author, and most began with no title at all. An author might intervene in the text to identify himself, or the scribe might identify the author of the text he copied, but many medieval saints' lives circulated with no authorial identification at all. It is not unusual then that, in the absence of any claim to authorship in the text itself, *Barlaam and Ioasaph* came to be associated with a famous Christian monk living in Palestine as it was copied and circulated.

The attribution of the Greek *Barlaam and Ioasaph* to John of Damascus was accepted for centuries, and it gave the story a prestige and authority it might not otherwise have had for medieval audiences. But as the transmission history of the story has become clearer, scholars have revisited the authorship of the Greek story. We now know that it is not an original composition based on an account brought by Indian Christians, as the story itself claims, or based on oral legends about the two saints. Moreover, John of Damascus is thought to have died in 749, long before the composition of the Greek *Barlaam and Ioasaph*, which we now know was a translation from the Georgian, completed in the late tenth or eleventh century.

But the identification of John of Damascus as the author of *Barlaam and Ioasaph*, although an enduring one, is not the only authorial identification in early manuscripts of the story. An alternative origin story for *Barlaam and Ioasaph* is found in an eleventh-century Greek manuscript and locates the composition of the story not in Palestine but in Greece, and at another famous monastery, Mount Athos.

## Euthymius the Iberian

In this manuscript, John is not the story's author but its courier. John is one of the "devout men from the inner land of the Ethiopians, whom our tale calls Indians," and he brings the story from Ethiopia to Jerusalem. The manuscript goes on to report that the story was translated from Georgian into Greek by Euthymius the Iberian. Why the Ethiopian or Indian John was known as John of St. Sabas is not explained, nor is why he would bring a tale written in Georgian from Ethiopia or India.

Euthymius the Iberian, also known as Euthymius of Athos, lived in the late tenth and early eleventh centuries in the Georgian monastery of Iviron, founded on Mount Athos in Greece in 980. He became its abbot in 1005. Most of what we know about Euthymius comes from a biography written by his more famous fellow Georgian priest, George of Athos—also known as George the Hagiorite—who records that Euthymius translated the *Balavariani* from Georgian into Greek. An anonymous translator of the story from Greek into Latin in 1048 also states that the work was translated by a monk named Eufimius from Abkhazia, a kingdom in the Caucasus that became part of the kingdom of Georgia in 1008. Thus, both works point to Euthymius as the redactor of the Greek *Barlaam and Ioasaph*, and both identify the Greek text as a translation from Georgian rather than a transcription, in Greek, of an oral account from Indian Christians. While we now know that *Barlaam and Ioasaph* was indeed translated from Georgian into Greek, we do not know with certainty that it was translated by Euthymius. Modern scholars tend to think of it as an anonymous work, translated by a monk whose name was not preserved.

In fact, Euthymius was best known as a translator of Greek texts into Georgian, and he is thought to have translated more than one hundred sixty biblical and patristic texts. Such translations made texts in the learned language of the church accessible to those who did not know Greek. Euthymius is not known to have translated Georgian texts into Greek, although there is no reason that he could not have.

While Georgian was spoken by monks in Palestine and in Greece, it was still a regional language. Translation into Greek vastly expanded the audience for the story of the two saints. The language of the Church also gave authority to the story of the pious prince's conversion of India. The erroneous identification of John of Damascus as its author further endorsed its veracity.

The translation is also a rewriting. As we noted above, the Greek text has an extended prologue and a brief epilogue not found in the Georgian version. Three of the parables found in the Georgian text have been eliminated in the Greek text, including the tale of the amorous wife told by the king. But for any reader of the two versions, the most striking difference is that the Greek version is full of passages from scripture and from the writings of the Church Fathers, especially John of Damascus. Scholars have not always appreciated the changes in the Greek text; the nineteenth-century scholar Joseph Jacobs called them "dogmatic colouring," and saw the interpolations as the translator's misplaced display of his theological learning. In the opinion of a modern Georgian scholar, speaking from a somewhat partisan perspective, "From the point of view of literary artistry, the Greek version is inferior to the Georgian."[4]

If the anonymous Georgian monks Christianized the Arabic tale, the Greek monk theologized it. The speeches are more formal and formulaic; the meanings of the parables are expounded with scriptural citation and ecclesiastical exegesis. One of the most significant changes, and certainly the most extensive addition of theological doctrine, is found when the debate between the Christians and idolaters is rewritten as a discourse on Christian belief. The Georgian story recounts King Abenes's attempt to deceive his son by staging a debate between the representatives from the idolatrous religion and the disguised Nakhor rather succinctly: "Nakhor opened his lips and began to denounce the idols and their acolytes and then to praise the faith of the Christians and their sacred laws." In the Greek text, the idol worshippers are identified as Greeks and Egyptians who worship many gods, Chaldeans who venerate the elements, and Jews who do not recognize Christ. The disguised Nakhor challenges each religion in succession, scornfully explaining its errors and extolling Christian truth, with frequent reference to scripture. Although Greeks, Egyptians, and Chaldeans might be called idolaters from a Christian perspective—and thus plausibly represent the religion of the king—Jews cannot be called idolaters. And Greeks, Egyptians, and Chaldeans strangely disappear from the story after they appear in the debate. The elaboration of the debate episode in the Greek *Barlaam and Ioasaph* seems out of place, and in fact it is.

## The Apology of Aristides

Church historians had long known of the *Apology of Aristides*, a lost work mentioned in the fourth century by Eusebius, Bishop of Caesarea, and in the early fifth century by the Latin priest and theologian Jerome, best known for his translation of the Bible into Latin and later recognized as a saint. Eusebius and Jerome report that Aristides was a philosopher from Athens who continued to wear his philosopher's robes after his conversion to Christianity. When Hadrian came to Athens in 125 CE for the annual celebration of the Eleusinian Mysteries, Aristides was granted an audience with the emperor and presented his *Apology*, a defense of Christianity as a philosophy superior to other religions. Aristides explained that there are four peoples in the world: Barbarians, Greeks (a category he uses also to include Chaldeans and Egyptians), Jews, and Christians. He then described the beliefs and practices of each, arguing that Christianity is both ethically and philosophically superior to them all. The emperor was apparently sufficiently impressed to issue an order that Christians were not to be prosecuted without a proper investigation and trial. The *Apology of Aristides* gained substantial fame in late antiquity; Eusebius reports the existence of many copies during his own time. However, after Jerome, the work is rarely mentioned, and it came to be regarded as one of the great lost works of the patristic period.

We now need to move forward more than fourteen hundred years after Jerome's fifth-century account. On the small island of San Lazzaro in the Venetian lagoon is the monastery of the

Mechitarists, founded by a congregation of Benedictine monks from Armenia. In 1878, the monks of the monastery published two chapters of the *Apology of Aristides*, translated from Armenian into Latin. The text's authenticity was immediately dismissed by the leading biblical scholar of the day, Ernest Renan. But in 1889, the Cambridge scholar Rendel Harris discovered a Syriac version of the text in the Monastery of St. Catherine on Mount Sinai. He published a critical edition of the text with an English translation, which was read by another Cambridge scholar, J. A. Robinson, who felt he had seen it somewhere before. Robinson had read the *Apology* in *Barlaam and Ioasaph* and was the first to realize that the text had been extant for centuries and in an only slightly abbreviated form in the Greek version of our story. The eloquent defense of Christianity spoken by the pagan magician disguised as Barlaam is in fact the *Apology of Aristides*.

As reproduced by Euthymius the Iberian (or whoever the Greek author might have been), the debate is significantly expanded, offering a lengthy defense of the Christian faith and a refutation of the beliefs of pagans, here identified as Greeks, Egyptians, and Chaldeans, and of the Jews. The *Apology*, like the extensive citations from the Bible and the Church Fathers, gives the story a tone of high Christian seriousness; at times it reads like a theological treatise.

Like the Georgian *Balavariani*, the Greek *Barlaam and Ioasaph* concludes with the prince's retirement from the world and his rejection of worldly pursuits, but the Greek version also extends and further Christianizes that ending. As we saw earlier, the Arabic *Bilawhar and Būdhāsaf* recounts the death of the prince in terms that recall the Buddha's passage into nirvana. The Georgian *Balavariani* describes the death of a Christian hermit: Iodasaph dwells at the tomb of his teacher Balahvar, he dreams of his future glory, and then he dies. Both hermits' bodies are brought back to Iodasaph's former kingdom and installed in a church where a great many miracles occur.

The Greek text expands the narrative of Ioasaph's death. We learn that Ioasaph leaves his kingdom when he is twenty-five years old and that he dwells in the wilderness for thirty-five years. When Ioasaph dies, he receives the crown of glory that has been prepared for him. A hermit comes to care for Ioasaph's body, performs Christian rites, and buries the body alongside Barlaam's. King Barachias comes to retrieve the bodies and finds them rosy and uncorrupted, a sign of their sanctity. He carries them back to his kingdom in a solemn procession and they are interred in a church, which becomes the site of miraculous cures and other wonders. Indeed, although the Greek *Barlaam and Ioasaph* is pervaded by a markedly theological tone, it is more likely that narrative developments like these established its enduring popularity in subsequent centuries. Medieval audiences seem to have had a great appetite for accounts of struggles that led to sanctity, and whether they extolled the asceticism of hermit saints, the abject bodily practices of anchorites, or the heroic resistance of martyr saints to tyrannical pagan rulers, narratives about the lives of the saints were immensely popular, particularly in vernacular translations. But before *Barlaam and Josaphat* could become a medieval blockbuster, the Greek text had to be translated into Latin.

## Greek to Latin

The first Latin translation of our story was made in 1047 or 1048 by monks in Amalfi who were in close contact with Byzantium; they likely acquired a copy of the Greek text relatively soon after its translation from Georgian.[5] A single manuscript of this translation survives and does not seem to have circulated widely or to have been translated into any other language. By contrast, a second Latin translation from the Greek, made a little later, probably in the twelfth century, had a vast diffusion and survives in sixty-two manuscripts in libraries throughout Europe. It was the basis for subsequent Latin versions of the story and was the version translated into European vernacular languages. The story was inevitably changed through translation, as we have seen from its earliest forms. Translators "modernized" the story with contextual details from their own cultures, adding new episodes or, alternatively, condensing the story, as in a thirteenth-century French version in which all the parables are omitted.

*Barlaam and Josaphat* was translated into Latin at a time when saints' lives, or *vitae*, were extremely popular. The saints whose life stories circulated in medieval Europe were holy men and women who lived lives of extraordinary virtue and had been granted entrance to the kingdom of heaven.[6] The earliest Christian saints were martyrs who died during persecutions of the new religion. After the conversion of the Roman emperor Constantine in 313, other forms of sanctity began to be recognized, in particular that of men and some women who left the privileges of the secular world to live in desolate places and devote themselves to ascetic practices. The stories of these saints' lives were strongly didactic: they taught and promoted monastic practices, the renunciation of the secular world, and the turn toward heaven. Narrative accounts of these so-called "confessor" saints—so called because they confessed or taught Christian faith—began to circulate as early as the fourth and fifth centuries CE and had an enduring influence on Christian hagiography.

Some saints, such as the apostles, were universally recognized; others had local followings that sometimes gained influence and spread more broadly or, alternatively, failed to garner broader attention and were forgotten. Saints were celebrated on a feast day that marked the day of the saint's death and rebirth in heaven; most were venerated by communities of believers, and their cults endured by tradition rather than by official ecclesiastical sanction. Papal control began to be exercised over the designation of sanctity in the eleventh century, but formal canonization processes were not instituted until later in the Middle Ages, and even then, there was no effort to remove saints who had appeared on the calendar of saints but who may never have lived beyond the pages of their pious stories. Barlaam and Josaphat were never formally canonized, but they appeared in the *Roman Martyrology* when it was published in 1583 by Pope Gregory XIII. The listing for November 27 reads: "Among the Indians, near the Persian boundary, the Saints Barlaam and Josaphat, whose wondrous deeds were written by St. John of Damascus."

Saints gained recognition and fame through accounts of the miracles accomplished by their relics and through the circulation of narratives about their lives. Beginning in the thirteenth century, saints' lives were used as didactic stories in the sermons preached by monks of mendicant orders like the Benedictines and Franciscans. Collections of exemplary stories were made for use by preachers and included saints' lives. The most famous and widely circulated among such collections was the *Golden Legend*, or *Legenda Aurea*, a Latin compilation that included an abridged translation of *Barlaam and Josaphat*.

## *The* Golden Legend

The *Golden Legend* was composed around 1260 by the Italian Benedictine Jacobus de Voragine, who was named archbishop of Genoa in 1292. Since the book was composed in Latin, it was probably intended for clerics, and since Jacobus belonged to the Benedictine preaching order, it was probably intended to provide material for preachers.[7] More than eight hundred manuscript copies of this compilation of saints' lives survive, and it was translated into or adapted in French, Occitan, Spanish, Italian, English, Dutch, High and Low German, and Bohemian.[8] The *Golden Legend* quickly took on a life of its own among lay readers. It continued to be popular after the invention of the printing press; before 1500, more editions of the *Golden Legend* were printed than of the Bible.

The "Story of Saints Barlaam and Josaphat" is attributed to John of Damascus in the *Golden Legend*.[9] It follows the established plot of the Greek story: a son is born to an idolatrous king who isolates him in a pleasure palace in an effort to avert a prophecy that he will leave his earthly kingdom to become a spiritual leader; the prince learns of Christianity from a hermit who teaches him using parables; the king tries to bring his son back to his pagan faith using persuasion, a staged dispute between pagan philosophers and a pagan disguised as the prince's Christian teacher, and, finally, the seductions of women. When his efforts fail, the king divides his kingdom and gives half to his son, who converts all his people and finally his father. The prince then retires to the desert to seek his master; they are reunited and both die in the wilderness. The *Golden Legend* emphasizes the "marvelous austerity" of the hermits; their willingness to embrace the privations of the desert to devote themselves to God earns them sanctity. After they die, their bodies are brought back into Josaphat's former kingdom, and many miracles occur at their shared tomb.

The narrator does not recount the miracles. In the *Golden Legend*, as in other examples of saints' lives, miracles are proof of sanctity; the fact that miracles occurred at the saints' tomb may be more important than what miracles occurred there. In the *Golden Legend*, the story of Barlaam and Josaphat is pared down to the essential elements of the plot and most of the didacticism is eliminated. Barlaam's lengthy explanations of Christian doctrine are absent. The story tells us that he taught Josaphat but preserves only the parables that illustrate his lessons, as in the following passage: "Barlaam then launched into a long sermon about the creation of the world, man's fall, the incarnation of the Son of God, his passion and resurrection, treating at length also about the Day of Judgment, the reward of the good, and the punishment of the wicked." Then the narrator recounts a parable found in all versions of the story.[10]

A hunter has captured a nightingale and is about to kill the bird when it speaks, asking him what he will gain by killing it, since the bird is too small to fill the hunter's belly. If the hunter will release him, the bird promises, it will give the hunter three pieces of advice that will bring him great advantages. The hunter agrees, and the nightingale tells him first, not to try to take possession of anything that is beyond his grasp; second, never to grieve over a lost thing that cannot be recovered; and third, never to believe the unbelievable. The hunter releases the bird and, as it flies away, the nightingale reproaches the hunter: he lost a precious thing because, the bird claims, it had a pearl larger than an ostrich egg in its belly. The hunter begins to lament and tries to recapture the nightingale. He is a fool, the bird reproaches, because he has not followed any of the advice the bird gave him. He tries to capture what he cannot attain, he grieves over what is irretrievably lost, and he believes that the bird's stomach can contain a pearl that would be larger than the bird's entire body. Barlaam's conclusion to the parable compares the foolishness of the gullible hunter to that of idolaters: "So those who trust in idols are fools, because they adore things that their own hands have shaped, and give the name of guardian to things they themselves must guard!"

The *Golden Legend* condenses Barlaam's teachings down to the parables and their meanings, and it abridges the lengthy debate between the pagan philosophers and Nachor, disguised as Barlaam; the entire *Apology of Aristides* added to the Greek translation is reduced to a single paragraph. What the redactor preserves are the stories—both the parables and the narrative action in Josaphat's story. He is more interested in illustrations of virtue than in lessons about virtue, and he is more interested in the trials and triumphs of the faithful than in discourses on doctrine. The *Golden Legend* recounts the king's attempt to have beautiful women seduce his son, using the parable about the boy raised in a cave to introduce the episode. The boy's attraction to women, "the demons who seduce men," above all other things, leads to the account of Josaphat's vulnerability to the seductions of the beautiful women his father sends to his palace. An evil spirit sent by the sorcerer Theodas inflames the young man, and when the demon sees that Josaphat wavers before the seductions of the articulate princess, he calls to his fellows, "You see how strongly that lass has shaken this man's resolution, while we haven't been able to shake him at all! Come, then! Let us find the right time and attack him with all our might!" God intervenes to bolster Josaphat's resolve to resist sexual temptation, and when the demons return in defeat to Theodas, he berates them for their failure. But they protest: "Before he made the sign of the cross, we assailed him and gave him much trouble, but once he had shielded himself with that sign, he came after us fully armed."

Throughout the *Golden Legend*, the compiler Jacobus de Voragine insists on the necessity of penance and on the desirability of earthly tribulation over wellbeing. As historian Sherry Reames has argued, Jacobus's theological imagination focused on conflict and adversity rather than on a loving God's relationship with his creatures. He insists on fortitude against the world and the importance of transcending earthly values and pleasures. The story of Barlaam and Josaphat provides him with ideal material, which he condenses into a series of efficient parables that teach the prince to disdain earthly values, seek his pleasures in heaven, and resist the demons that would corrupt his resolve. *Barlaam and Josaphat* does not receive any new interpretation in the *Golden Legend*, nor is its Christian message changed or intensified, but as part of a compilation that humanizes and dramatizes the lived experience of Christian doctrine, the legend of the pious prince and his teacher came alive for a broad readership.[11]

With its translation first into Greek and then into Latin, the story took the shape that it would retain for centuries, and introduced the names by which the protagonists would be known in subsequent translations of the story. The Georgian Iodasaph becomes the Greek Ioasaph, Balahvar becomes Barlaam, and King Abenes becomes King Abenner. When translated into Latin, the language shared by clerics throughout Europe, the legend became wildly popular. It circulated not only in the *Golden Legend* and vernacular translations of that collection, but also in translations of the longer Latin version. Some vernacular adaptations were abridged; others, like Gui de Cambrai's thirteenth-century Old French version, were greatly expanded. Just as the Buddha of the Indian tale had been transformed into a Christian prince, here the meek Christian prince of the Greek and Latin text will be transformed into a bellicose Crusader for Christ.

# CHAPTER FIVE

# The Pious Prince Goes to War:
# Gui de Cambrai's *Barlaam and Josaphat*

O ver the centuries, across two continents and several languages, our tale remains the story of conflict between a
father and son. A father loves his only son and seeks to ensure
his happiness, but his son seeks a different path, and so father
and son are at odds. It is a universal theme and for this reason,
perhaps, the legend was much translated. The father is also a
king and the son is his royal heir, making the story not just one
about how best to live, but how best to rule. However, the son
is destined for sanctity, making *Barlaam and Josaphat* also a
story about religion. Its adoption by three great religions also
suggests something universal, or at least trans-religious, about
its appeal.

The prince's renunciation of the demands and pleasures of
the world is represented as a rejection of his father and the life
he has led. The conflict between the father and his son takes
a variety of forms. In the story of the Buddha, the king and

his son disagree, but with loving words. The king does not dispute the wisdom of his son's decision to renounce the world, only its timing. In the Arabic version, the argument between father and son is more protracted and the words more heated. Still, both father and son claim to be disciples of the same prophet, al-Budd. The shared recognition of the prophet unites Būdhāsaf and King Junaysar even as they dispute the meaning and implications of al-Budd's teachings. In the Georgian adaptation al-Budd has disappeared, and the father's idolatry and the son's ascetic beliefs are more clearly in conflict. The opposition between idolatry and Christianity is accentuated in subsequent versions of the story, and it defines the relationship between the father and the son.

Although the outlines of the story remain highly consistent as it is translated and adapted over hundreds of years, the relationship between the father and the son evolves and changes in the different versions of *Barlaam and Josaphat*. The Georgian *Balavariani* represents King Abenes not just as a pagan but as a king "utterly immersed in the pursuit of the pleasures and delights of this world and enslaved by his own passions, and quite unable to exercise any restraint in respect of indulgences which are so pernicious to the soul." Believers in Christ and holy monks in his land detest the king's attachments to worldly pleasures and begin to preach about the transitory nature of the world and all its affairs. The king's reaction is notably political in the *Balavariani*: he fears the consequences of the Christians' teaching not just for his religion, nor even primarily for his religion, but for the wellbeing of his kingdom. In an exchange with Christian ascetics, he explains that he persecutes them because they set a dangerous example—if everyone were to renounce the world, society would collapse: "This wrath of mine serves as a lesson both for them and for the nation, so that the land may not become waste, and also to punish those ascetics for having no love for the good things of earth."[1]

The Georgian version of the story presents the king's persecution of Christians as a political decision: he fears social disorder and revolution. From Prince Iodasaph's perspective, the king's fear of the political consequences of Christianity's spread is another example of his father's failure to understand the transitory nature of the world and its pleasures. In the Greek version of the story (the immediate successor of the Georgian one), as in the Latin, the king's political concerns will be displaced through a purely religious wrath against Christian monastic orders. Yet the political nature of the conflict between religions would return, both in the story and in the uses of the story. The medieval versions of *Barlaam and Josaphat* preserve the conflation of religion and dynasty in the king's resistance to his son's conversion; some give a strong feudal structure to the king's relationship with his councilors and with his son. In his thirteenth-century French version of the story, Gui de Cambrai goes so far as to add a war between the king and the prince: the king reasons that if he cannot win his son by persuasion, he will defeat him in combat.[2] But as in the other versions of the story, the son triumphs over his father and the father becomes the son's disciple.

## Barlaam and Josaphat *in Thirteenth-Century France*

Gui de Cambrai has been identified as the author of at least one
other text, but we know little about him beyond what he himself tells us in his narratives.[3] Like other authors of the twelfth
and thirteenth centuries, he is known only by his first name
and a location; Cambrai is a region of northern France near the
Belgian border. His *Barlaam and Josaphat*, like other medieval
vernacular versions of the story, is translated from the Latin,
and Gui claims to work at the request of a patron. Because he
knew Latin, we assume that he was a cleric. He had literary
skills, or at least literary pretensions, since he translated from
Latin prose into Old French verse. He is also a highly opinion-
ated narrator, frequently interjecting himself into the story to
offer his perspective on events or characters, and sometimes
commenting on current affairs. He condemns the vices of
the nobility, the corruption of the church, and the cowardice
of those who have failed to go on crusades to win Jerusalem
from the Muslims. Gui's perspective is resolutely Christian:
he vilifies Jews and Muslims as pagans. And as in other medieval texts, the Jews come in for special blame; according to
Christian authors, their prophets foretold the coming of Christ
yet they refused to recognize him. Muslims are described as
idolaters like the Chaldeans, Greeks, and Egyptians whose
religions Nachor, the disguised Barlaam, refutes in the disputation staged by the king in an effort to convince his son to
abandon Christian belief.

"Idolater" is a fairly common term of abuse for Muslims
in medieval narratives, despite the fact that Islam forbids the

representation of living beings, and especially those of God and his prophets. The use of the term reveals both the limited knowledge of Islam among medieval Christians and the assumption that anyone who was not a Christian must be a pagan "idolater." "Saracen," the name commonly used for Muslims, also comes to have the general sense of "pagan." As we will see, Gui de Cambrai's *Barlaam and Josaphat* not only characterizes the prince's father as a Saracen but also pits Josaphat's Christians against the king's Saracen subjects in a holy war described using the rhetoric of Crusade propaganda.

Apart from the war episode, the story recounted in Gui de Cambrai's *Barlaam and Josaphat* is not significantly different from other versions of the story. However, the story's feudal vocabulary and the passages of social commentary pointedly addressed to a noble audience give the story a grounding in thirteenth-century culture despite its location in a faraway, rather vaguely located India. Gui's version is longer than many other medieval translations of the story, and not only because of the added episodes and the interventions he makes in his own voice. He also extends the characters' speeches, adding wordplay and puns, and uses elaborate metaphors to describe emotional states.

As in the Latin version that it translates, Gui de Cambrai's *Barlaam and Josaphat* begins with Josaphat's father, now called King Avenir. He is the rich and powerful ruler of India and he worships idols. Christianity has begun to take root in his realm, and he vows to rid his kingdom of all who would follow this faith. He persecutes the Christians viciously, but they do not fear the king's laws or prisons; they willingly suffer death for their faith. One of the king's own councilors becomes a Christian and abandons his family, his position at court, and all his wealth to live as a hermit in the wilderness. King Avenir is greatly sorrowed by his friend's desertion, and he summons him for an explanation. How could he abandon wealth, power, and comfort to live in such harsh conditions? The man admonishes the king for his greed and anger, and for his love of the world. He counsels him to renounce his possessions and wealth and to seek God. King Avenir responds by banishing his former councilor and renewing his persecution of Christians. He orders his men to kill all those Christians who remain in his lands.

The didactic tone of the story begins here—the king's councilor delivers a lesson in Christian doctrine that promotes the renunciation of the world. Like the *Golden Legend*, Gui's *Barlaam and Josaphat* is written for a secular audience, but it does not abridge the text as Jacobus de Voragine does. It preserves the extensive lessons in Christian doctrine, closely following the didacticism of the Greek version as it was translated into Latin. Yet it popularizes those lessons, putting them into verse couplets and adopting the conventions of vernacular literary genres. The description of the king's plot to have his son seduced by beautiful women calls on the vocabulary of courtly love, and portraits of Prince Josaphat echo romance descriptions of valiant knights. Gui de Cambrai's *Barlaam and Josaphat* was clearly meant to be read, and likely read aloud, over many days or evenings. The presentations of Christian doctrine probably confirmed the noble audience's faith, but not so much as to inspire any of its members to abandon their estates for an ascetic's life in the wilderness. In fact, Gui's interventions in the story tell his audience how they should interpret its lessons: they should be generous to the poor and not disdain those of lesser rank. They should devote themselves to God rather than the pleasures of the world, but by changing their habits in this world, not by abandoning it for a life in the wilderness.

## Barlaam's Lessons

As in earlier versions of the story, in Gui's *Barlaam and Josaphat*, the story of the Buddha's birth and youth is repeated in the account of the king's desire for a son, the birth of Josaphat, the prediction of his future, his isolation in a pleasure palace, and his excursions into the city where he sees a sick man, an infirm man, and an old man. The troubled Josaphat longs for teachings that will help him understand the world. And as in the earlier versions, here *Barlaam and Josaphat* departs from the Buddha's story: a teacher arrives. God understands Josaphat's longing for truth and sends the hermit Barlaam to him. Gui's version of the legend follows its Latin model closely in the sequence of parables that Barlaam uses to teach the king's son about Christianity and to exhort him to place his faith in God.

One of Barlaam's lessons is that greed inevitably corrupts relationships in the secular world, and he recounts a parable to illustrate that faith in the values of this world will always be betrayed.[4] A king had a trusted steward and entrusted a large part of the country to his authority, Barlaam tells Josaphat.

The steward, who accepted the land and managed it for his lord, had three friends. He loved and cherished two of them more than the third. He shared his wealth with the two friends and made them great lords. He wanted them to love him and compromised himself to please them and advance their interests. He broke vows and lied for them; he wronged many people and even had some put to death for the sake of his friends. He was less generous with the third man, whom he distrusted because he was an intimate of the king.

One day the king summoned his steward for a reckoning. He had managed the king's land for a long time, and the king desired an account of how he had used the country's wealth. The steward was afraid, since he had given the king's profits to his friends. He went to them to ask for their help. The first friend sent him away, saying that he had found new friends and no longer cared for the steward. The second friend also sent him away, saying that he was busy with other affairs. The steward was desperate. He did not expect the third friend to help him, since the first two would not and he had been less generous to the third. But he finally went to his third friend. He bowed before him without pride and begged his forgiveness. The friend welcomed the steward and offered to go to court with him and reconcile him with the king. The steward marveled at his friend's generosity and forgiveness: "I am surprised that this man for whom I did nothing is willing to sacrifice himself and everything he possesses for my sake. He gave me more than I asked for, and he has proven himself a true friend."

Barlaam explains the meaning of the parable to Josaphat.

The first friend represents wealth, he says, but wealth and power are lost when a man dies. The second friend represents pride, which is also lost when a man dies. The third friend represents the good deeds of the Christian. "These are the three friends the steward found in the world," Barlaam explains. "Two of them kill and condemn him, but the goodness of the third redeems him. Two lead him to sorrow, the third earns him the love of the king he betrayed. The third friend remains with him and reconciles him with his lord, who is full of mercy. Shun the first two friends," Barlaam says to Josaphat, "and take good care of the third, for whoever neglects the first two and serves the third will save his soul." Good deeds endure, Barlaam teaches, whereas wealth and pride will fade away, and in this parable, as in others, the difference is emphasized in a story about human bonds. Love for other human creatures, whether father or friend, must be secondary to love for God. This lesson receives its most emphatic expression in another episode that echoes scenes from the life of the Buddha: the account of the king's efforts to win back his son using the sexual seductions of beautiful women.

## Flesh and Spirit

Even before the full transmission history of *Barlaam and Josaphat* was known, three episodes were cited as evidence that the medieval saint's life was based on the life of the Buddha: the prediction of the astrologers, the chariot rides, and the beautiful women's efforts to seduce the prince. Most attention has been given to the chariot rides, where the prince first encounters old age, sickness, and death. Here there is clear evidence for the influence of the Buddha's story, although, as we noted in Chapter One, the chariot scene does not appear at all in the works that scholars regard as the earliest renditions of the life of the Buddha. The episode in which the king instructs beautiful women to seduce his son has received the least comment, perhaps because the episode is less formulaic than the other two. There are also significant differences both among the various Buddhist versions and between the Muslim and Christian versions. In addition, there are differences between the Buddhist versions and the Barlaam corpus; the most striking is that conversion plays no role in the Buddhist narrative but is central to the Muslim and Christian versions. Not only does a beautiful princess try to seduce the prince, but she also offers to convert to his religion if he will make love to her.

In both the Buddha and Barlaam stories, desire for the world and attachment to worldly pleasures take many forms: the comforts of a well-appointed home, an abundant table, luxurious clothing, power, distinction, and privilege. For our male protagonists, one of the most tenacious attractions of the world is sexual desire for a woman. Lovely women's bodies that would ensnare the prince in worldly desire are elements of the material world, and like the world, they must be rejected. The notion that women threaten men by inspiring sexual desire is not limited to *Barlaam and Josaphat* and the life of the Buddha. It appears in Christian, Muslim, and Buddhist literature during many historical periods. Yet the equation of women with the temptations of the material world receives a particularly rich representation in our stories, where the contest for the prince's soul is won only when he comes to see women as abject, disgusting, and even diabolical.

In *Barlaam and Josaphat*, as in the earlier Arabic *Bilawhar and Būdhāsaf*, the king's councilor Theodas convinces King Avenir that Josaphat's stubborn opposition to his father's religion can be overcome if he will replace his son's male servants and courtiers with women. The women will seduce Josaphat so that he will abandon his harsh beliefs and return to the pleasures of the world and his father's religion. In order to convince the king that men are always vulnerable to the enchantments of women, Theodas recounts the story of the king's son who will die if light reaches his eyes before he is twelve years old. The son is raised in a dark cave, and when the boy's isolation from the world ends, he is taken out into the world and taught to name the things that inhabit it. When he sees women for the first time in his life and asks what they are called, his courtiers answer that these are devils that deceive men. Upon the prince's return to his castle, his father asks what sight pleased him most. The boy replies that he loved nothing as much as these devils.

As we noted earlier, the fable about the boy raised in a cave is found in the Arabic *Bilawhar and Būdhāsaf*; it is preserved in subsequent translations of the legend and taken up by later writers for other uses. Boccaccio uses it in the *Decameron* in the introduction to the fourth day of stories, though there the boy is told that the women are called geese, not devils. The most obvious lesson of the story would seem to be the arbitrary relationship between words and the things they name, since women will deceive men no matter what they are called, or so the story goes. But in the Barlaam texts, as in other uses of the story, the lesson the fable offers is not about the nature of language, or even about naming women (hence the variability of the story: they are called devils or geese), but about the nature of desire: men will always desire women, even if they do not know what to call them, for "nature cannot lie," as Gui de Cambrai puts it. The fable further suggests that this desire gives women power over men, and that is the key to Theodas's plot to bring Josaphat back into the enjoyment of worldly pleasures.

Of all the exemplary stories in *Barlaam and Josaphat*, the parable about the boy in the cave is the only one that repeats elements of Josaphat's own story. He too is raised in isolation from the world, but in Josaphat's case, the women he encounters really are "devils that deceive men." They are inspired by Satan, the narrator tells us in some versions of the story, or in other versions, they are possessed by demons.

According to Theodas's plan, beautiful highborn young women are placed in Josaphat's household. They speak so enticingly to him that he will sin, Gui de Cambrai explains, if he does not fight against nature. A beautiful princess approaches Josaphat and promises to convert to Christianity if Josaphat will marry her and take her virginity. Josaphat refuses her bargain. To join his body with hers would be to corrupt himself. "I will not defile myself with such a base partner," he tells her. The prince's characterization of sexual union as a defilement derives from the valorization of sexual continence that is a theme of Barlaam's lessons. It also corresponds to the monastic valorization of virginity. But when Josaphat claims that he must preserve his virginity, the princess responds with a defense of marriage: "Are Christians defiled when they take women as wives?" she asks. She then uses the Scriptures to argue for the legitimacy of marriage. "God himself commanded it, and He joined together the first man and woman," she continues. "Saint Paul himself confirms that I do not lie when I say that it is much better for a man to marry than for his body to burn forever." Josaphat concedes that marriage is permitted to Christians, but argues for the superiority of virginity. The princess then reminds Josaphat that Saint Peter and the prophets married and they were not damned for it. She claims that he is a bad Christian if he will not follow Christian law and marry her to save her soul, but she cannot persuade the prince to abandon his resolve. She then concedes, in part. Since Josaphat will not marry her, let him spend only one night with her, and she will convert; he can save her by making love to her only once. At his refusal, she complains, "My Christianity would be your salvation, for if I were saved by you, you would have done a good deed and the reward would belong to you alone. But you are a harsh Christian."

The princess's bargain defines sexual intercourse as a virtuous act. The question of conversion turns the prince's decision into a dilemma different from the choice between enjoying sexual pleasure and renouncing it. That is, the decision to succumb to the women's seductions or resist them is complicated by the choice between saving the princess's soul or, as she claims, damning it. Although Josaphat refuses the princess's bargain, he remains torn between pity for the princess and fear of sin. He thinks that he will wrong God if he does not do as she asks, but he fears that he will anger God if he complies. He goes into another room and kneels in prayer. He falls asleep while praying and in his dream the Archangel Michael takes his soul to heaven to see its pleasures and then to hell to see the torments suffered by those disloyal to God. Michael also reveals King Avenir's deception to Josaphat. The prince wakes, and Gui de Cambrai tells us that "he shuddered from fear" as he remembers the horrors of hell.

Josaphat then falls ill, and it is not clear whether his sickness comes from his distress at his father's betrayal, the fear inspired by the vision of hell, or the fear of losing God's love. At this point in the story, we see another difference between the Buddhist and Christian versions. In the story of the Buddha, the prince leaves the palace shortly after the seduction scene, but in the Christian version he remains, and, following the advice of his advisor, Aracis, King Avenir makes another attempt to attach his son to the world: if Josaphat cannot be seduced by its pleasures, let him be shaped by its travails. King Avenir will divide his lands and give Josaphat half his kingdom. An effective ruler must compromise his principles to govern; the prince will be faced with difficulties and he will inevitably make unjust decisions. King Josaphat will not be able to maintain the pious resolve of Prince Josaphat.

The seduction episode is a pivotal moment in the Christian version of the story. It leads to the founding of Josaphat's Christian realm, the subsequent conversion of his father, and Josaphat's reunion with Barlaam in the desert. Just as the Buddha's disdain for the beautiful women's bodies leads him to leave the palace, heralding his enlightenment six years later, so the seduction episode moves the Barlaam story toward its resolution. It is the moment at which the story turns away from Josaphat's own conversion and toward the conversion of his people and the building of a Christian kingdom.

## King Josaphat

When King Avenir tells Josaphat of his decision to give him half his kingdom, Josaphat initially resists but then realizes that if he agrees, he can escape his father and follow his own beliefs. King Avenir organizes a great coronation ceremony and after two months of festivities, he crowns Josaphat and sends him into his new country. Josaphat finds it to be a beautiful land, prosperous and fertile; its people are industrious and welcome their new king. But this new land is filled with idols.

Josaphat immediately begins to destroy them all. He converts the people through his exhortations, his preaching, and the example he sets. Gui de Cambrai reports that John of Damascus himself arrives to serve as archbishop in Josaphat's capital city. It is he who will later record Josaphat's story, Gui adds, in an endorsement of the long tradition that identifies John as the author of the story. The archbishop baptizes the converts and leads them as they pull down the altars to idols and build churches. The country prospers, the entire kingdom is converted, and people from neighboring lands also turn to Christianity. Many of King Avenir's own people become Christians, and many of his courtiers and councilors desert him. Josaphat has established a Christian realm.

King Avenir is increasingly incensed by the prosperity of

Josaphat's kingdom, which flourishes as his own declines. The duties of kingship have not led Josaphat to abandon Christianity, as his father had expected, and many of King Avenir's own subjects have left him to practice his son's faith. In most versions of *Barlaam and Josaphat*, the king then begins to feel remorse for his persecution of Christians. He converts and spends the rest of his days in repentance. However, in Gui de Cambrai's version, the end of the story is greatly expanded. In a long development found only in Gui's version of the legend, King Avenir goes to war against his son.

Avenir summons the councilors who have not deserted him and presents his plan, which they endorse: if he cannot win his son through persuasion, he will go to war to take back his lands and force his son to return to his father's religion. Aracis especially encourages him to reclaim his lands from Josaphat, and the king reminds his councilor that he was following Aracis's advice when he divided his kingdom in the first place. Aracis admits his error and promises to support the king, as do his other vassals. King Avenir then summons all his allies and sends word to his son: if Josaphat will not renounce his crown and his kingdom, he should prepare to defend himself, for the king will attack Josaphat's city, capture it, and restore the old religion. Josaphat refuses to give up his land. He has taken it from Avenir's false gods and he will defend it for the true God he serves.

Josaphat seeks the counsel of the archbishop and his vassals. The archbishop declares that King Avenir challenges the divine law that Josaphat has established. In a speech reminiscent of the propaganda used to recruit knights to recapture the Holy Land from the infidels, the archbishop encourages the king: "You have enough people to defend this land and it should not be given up to the Saracens. They will install their idols here and bring down the Holy Church. My lord, you have converted this land through much pain and effort, but you will see it revert to evil if you give it to your father. The country will be lost to God, who made you its lord." The archbishop calls the lords of the city to a holy war. Although in *Barlaam and Josaphat* the Christian knights will go to war to defend their own land and not to win land from an enemy, the archbishop's exhortation to fight evokes the Crusaders' call to take up the cross and win Jerusalem and the holy lands of Palestine.

In 1095 Pope Urban II preached the First Crusade to a fervent and enthusiastic response, and by 1099 Christian troops had captured Jerusalem, Antioch, Edessa, Tripoli, and Tyre. During the twelfth century the Crusaders established four Christian states in Palestine, but continuing losses, including the fall of Edessa in 1144 and the loss of Jerusalem in 1187, meant that the Crusades did not end in victory. French nobles were leaders of the early Crusades, and French literary texts celebrated their victories in epic narratives about kings and counts who went to battle against the Saracens to win land and honor for France and for God. "Pagans are wrong and Christians are right" is a line repeated in one of the most famous of these epics, the *Song of Roland*, and while Josaphat's archbishop does not use precisely this phrase, he certainly embraces its meaning.

Josaphat arms his people and organizes the defense of his city. Meanwhile King Avenir's vassals assemble from far and wide, and they march on Josaphat's land. They set up their tents, place their idols on altars, and storm the city. Josaphat's archers fire arrows from the ramparts, and the battle begins. The archbishop exhorts the Christians to fight well. In fact, he takes up the sword himself. His fierce fighting recalls that of Archbishop Turpin in the *Song of Roland*, which Gui de Cambrai was likely to have known. In this account of the battle between Charlemagne's nephew Roland and the Saracens who attack him as he travels over the Pyrenees from Spain to France, Archbishop Turpin is a warrior priest and exhorts his men to fight for God. Like Turpin, the archbishop in *Barlaam and Josaphat* shows a zeal and prowess that inspire the Christian knights, as the narrator emphasizes: "He knew that if the battle were not won, Christianity would be lost. He fought well and broke many mail shirts; he split many helms and killed many pagans in the battle. His blood-drenched sword was twisted and dented, and his damaged shield had taken at least a hundred blows. He fought with courage, as did the entire army." The knights fight to save Christianity and a Christian land, the land that Josaphat and the archbishop have converted.

The story relates a series of encounters between brave knights from each side, and descriptions of the battles draw on the narrative model of medieval epic poems about war, often against Muslims. Many men are killed, many are captured, and as night falls, Josaphat has the advantage. A three-day truce is declared to allow each side to bury its dead and care for its wounded. The men captured by Josaphat convert to Christianity, and his people rejoice to find that the number of their allies lost in battle has been replenished by the converts.

King Avenir curses his gods and sends for more men to replace the dead. His councilor Aracis promises to win the city for him. When the battle resumes, Aracis contrives to be captured by Josaphat's men, and once he is inside the Christian city, he pretends to convert. He demonstrates enthusiastic piety, refusing to leave his prayers and spending all his time prostrate before an image of the crucified Christ. He earns the trust of Josaphat and the archbishop and is given command of the highest and strongest tower in the city. From there he sends word to Josaphat's father that he will deliver the city to him. Avenir's men should advance silently and Aracis will open the gates. Once they have occupied the tower, they will easily be able to take the city.

King Avenir rejoices at this news and vows to follow Aracis's instructions. However, one of his vassals is disturbed by the plan. He is a secret Christian and does not wish to see Josaphat's kingdom fall. Like so many others in the story, he is torn between two masters. King Avenir is his lord, and he should not betray him. Yet he will betray his God if he is complicit in the plot against Josaphat. Law and custom demand that he should remain loyal to his lord, but then he thinks that he should have greater faith in God than in the laws of man. Finally deciding that he should display more loyalty to a heavenly king than to a temporal one, the vassal sends word to Josaphat of Aracis's betrayal. Forewarned of the plan, Josaphat's watchman sounds an alarm when Avenir's men approach and Aracis opens the gate for them. King Avenir's men flee, and Aracis retreats into the tower where he is captured and executed, condemned because he pledged himself to God and then betrayed Him. After this ultimate defeat, King Avenir finally recognizes the truth of his son's faith, converts, and spends the rest of his days in repentance.

Gui de Cambrai portrays King Avenir's decision to go to war against Josaphat's Christian kingdom as a crusade precisely at the time that Crusades were taking Christians into Muslim lands. In Gui's story the positions are reversed: the invader is not the Christian but the Muslim. Still, the parallel between the war in the story and the war in the world is suggested not just by Gui's characterization of King Avenir's allies as Saracens but also by the use of narrative conventions from stories about the wars against the Saracens. As if all this were not clear enough, the narrator intervenes in his text to lament the fate of the holy city of Jerusalem, and to excoriate noblemen who vowed to take up the cross but broke their promises.

By the early 1220s, when Gui de Cambrai was composing his *Barlaam and Josaphat*, Western Christians had been at war in Palestine for over a century. At the end of the twelfth century, the Third Crusade regained some of the territory the Christians had seized in early victories, although the Crusaders did not win back the holy city of Jerusalem. The Fourth Crusade never even reached Palestine, since its leaders became embroiled in the politics of the Byzantine empire. In 1204, after their armies had been stranded outside of Constantinople without the payments promised by the Byzantine emperor, they sacked the Christian city, including the cathedral of Hagia Sofia. They looted not just the material riches of the imperial city but also precious Christian relics, including a fragment of the True Cross.

By the thirteenth century, new fronts had opened in the Crusaders' battle, some on European soil: Christians were fighting against the Slavs on the Baltic coast, the Moors in Spain, and heretical Cathars in the south of France. There was relative peace in Palestine due to a truce with the Muslims, but anticipating the end of that truce and wishing to concentrate Christian military efforts in the east, Pope Innocent III began preaching a new crusade in 1213. The Fifth Crusade was not popular with French nobles, perhaps because they had been so deeply involved with the Albigensian Crusade against the Cathars in southern France, and they remained relatively indifferent to the call to take up the cross. The Fifth Crusade ended in a disastrous defeat for the Christians in Egypt in 1221.[5]

When Gui de Cambrai reproaches noblemen who neglect what he calls their duty to take up the cross and take back the Holy Land, he may be recalling the weak response among Frenchmen to the Fifth Crusade, or he may anticipate future wars in Palestine. Whatever his reference, he clearly promotes the mandate for Christians to regain Jerusalem and rewrites *Barlaam and Josaphat* to serve this purpose. The conflict between the pagan father and his ascetic son found in all versions of the story here escalates into a holy war in which Christian knights successfully defend a land devoted to God against pagans who would defile it. In Gui's narrative, the pious Josaphat is not only a spiritual leader but also a soldier of God.

## Body and Soul

King Avenir lives only a few years after his conversion. When he dies, Josaphat declares that he has fulfilled his duties in the present world since he has led his father to Christianity and his father's people to the true faith. He intends to leave the throne and go into the wilderness to join his master, Barlaam, as he promised. Josaphat calls for Barachie, the single Christian who long before had attended the disputation between Nachor, disguised as Barlaam, and King Avenir's priests and philosophers. King Josaphat gives his crown to Barachie and sets out to join Barlaam in his hermitage. Josaphat's people are alarmed, protesting that he must stay to lead them in the ways of the Lord. They fear that if he leaves, the land will fall back into paganism. Josaphat reassures them that they have already learned much about Christianity and Barachie will be a good king and lead them well. But Barachie himself refuses the crown. Why should he wear it if Josaphat will not? Barachie joins the people in their refusal to allow Josaphat to depart, and they force him back to the palace.

When night falls, Josaphat takes off his rich clothing, puts on the hair shirt that Barlaam left for him, covers it with a simple mantle, and departs, leaving behind a letter to his people explaining his intention to seek Barlaam. But the people have kept watch and follow him, crying out with great laments, and once again they force him back to his palace. Josaphat insists that he will not rule, and his lords relent and ask him to give them a king who will keep his laws. Josaphat again calls Barachie forward. Josaphat assures him that he will be a good king, and this time the people accept Josaphat's decision, as does Barachie himself. The people and their new king accompany Josaphat for an entire day, and then turn back.

Josaphat continues into the wilderness, where he wanders for several years in search of Barlaam. He lives on roots, berries, and whatever he can find in the forest. He grows very thin, his skin turns dark from the sun, and his body suffers for the sake of his soul. At this point in the story, Gui de Cambrai adds another development to the text: a lengthy debate between personified figures of the Body and the Soul. Such debates were a widespread poetic genre in the Middle Ages and circulated in Latin and in vernacular languages. They represent a chastising Soul as seeking salvation through the renunciation of precisely those pleasures that the Body wants to enjoy.

The debate fittingly represents the struggle of the ascetic. In Gui de Cambrai's poem, the Body complains vociferously about lost comforts and pleasures: why must it suffer hunger and discomfort; why can it not continue to enjoy the rich food, the soft bed, the beautiful clothes, and all the other comforts to which it had grown accustomed? The Soul chastises the Body severely: its worldly pleasures harm the Soul, who seeks to save them both. The world and its pleasures will pass away, the Soul preaches, and so will the Body. It will die but it knows not when, and so Body and Soul must disdain the temporary pleasures of the present world and prepare for the next. The debate between his personified Body and Soul emphasizes the difficulty of the prince's renunciation; it also expands the pedagogical structure of the story. The Soul teaches the Body about salvation, and the Body finally agrees that it is better to suffer in the present than to be condemned to suffer for eternity.

Josaphat's soul triumphs over his body and he continues to wander in the wilderness, eating little, sleeping without shelter, and worshipping God. After two years, he comes upon a hermit who directs him to Barlaam. Josaphat and his teacher are reunited and they live together in devotion to God for many years. Then Barlaam dies, and angels carry his soul to heaven. Josaphat buries his master's body and sits on Barlaam's tomb. He does not eat or sleep, yet he is satisfied. He refuses all the pleasures of the world, prays, and reads the Scriptures.

Josaphat's example provokes a long lament by the narrator about the sins of the present world. He describes the corruption of the clergy, the suffering of the poor, and the lack of faith among noblemen. Again, he excoriates those noblemen who took up the cross but shirked the Crusades. Even those who participated in the Crusades do not escape Gui's wrath. He lambasts them for failing to win the cities of Palestine for the Christians. "The command that you should go to Damascus to conquer the pagans has been issued. What will you do with your cross? You should have taken it to the Holy Sepulchre long ago, but you loved your own country too much. The pleasures and delights of the world overwhelm you and you reject the good path that promises you the highest joy! You are consumed by the sin that holds you hostage." It is perhaps not surprising that a thirteenth-century author would imagine the conflict between a Christian kingdom and a pagan kingdom in the language of the Crusades. Gui speaks directly to his own time and place, unleashing invective against the knights who failed to reclaim the Holy Land. The language Gui uses to condemn his cowardly compatriots clearly echoes the language that the Christian ascetic prince uses to condemn the pagan idolaters. For Gui de Cambrai, Josaphat's successful defense of his city and his lands as well as his defeat and conversion of the idolatrous King Avenir and his subjects are models for Christian knights and an admonishment to those who have refused to go into battle to reclaim the Holy Land.

## The Afterlife of the Saint

After spending thirty-five years as a hermit, Josaphat dies. He did not spend his days in vain, the narrator tells us. He refrained from sin and desired the good, he saved many souls from the devil, and he set an example for us. After Josaphat's death, God sends a hermit to perform the death rituals and bury Josaphat with Barlaam, his companion in the search for God. Then God sends the hermit to India to take word of Josaphat's death to King Barachie. The king hastens to the tomb with a great company of people, and they weep in sorrow. When they open the tomb, they find Josaphat and Barlaam lying side by side. They have become healthy and whole; their bodies have a sweet fragrance and have not decomposed, a sign of God's grace and of their sanctity. Barachie has the bodies transported back to Josaphat's city, where they are enshrined in the church Josaphat himself had built to honor God. The sick and infirm come from near and far and are healed. Pagans learn of the miracles and they convert.

Barlaam and Josaphat die, but their bodies are venerated as miracle-working relics. After the death of the Buddha, his body was cremated and his relics distributed among his followers, who enshrined them in *stūpas*. The relics of Barlaam and Josaphat were less widely distributed but, according to believers, no less precious. In 1571, the Doge of Venice presented a bone from Josaphat's spine to King Sebastian of Portugal; the bone is enshrined today in Saint Andrieskerk in Antwerp.

Barlaam and Josaphat also live on through their story, of course. By the time that Gui de Cambrai's audience heard it, the legend had been in circulation for five centuries. Originally a Buddhist story, it had been appropriated by Muslim, then Christian writers. But the story had another trajectory as well. About the same time that Gui de Cambrai was translating the Latin Christian version into Old French, a Jewish writer in Iberia translated the Arabic *Bilawhar and Būdhāsaf* into Hebrew.

## The Prince and the Hermit

In 711, Muslim armies from North Africa invaded the Iberian Peninsula. By 720, Muslims controlled nearly the entire peninsula, and Iberia became Al-Andalus, a province of the Umayyad caliphate. Under Muslim rule, Christians and Jews were allowed to practice their own religion and lived as *dhimmī*, non-Muslim citizens of an Islamic state. Although the majority of the population of Al-Andalus remained Christian, there was a significant Jewish presence in the region. Modern scholars have challenged the pervasive notion that Christians, Jews, and Muslims lived harmoniously in medieval Iberia; we know, for example, that there were persecutions of Jews in eleventh-century Córdoba and Granada. Yet cultural exchange was lively, and translations of Arabic philosophical and scientific texts transformed the intellectual world of medieval Europe.

Only a small area in the north of Iberia remained under Christian control after the Muslim conquest, and over the course of the Middle Ages, the Christians of Iberia gradually regained power and expelled the Muslims from the peninsula.

This process, known as the *Reconquista*, was completed during the reign of Ferdinand and Isabella. In the famous year of 1492, Muhammad XII, king of Granada, surrendered to the Catholic monarchs. That same year the Christians expelled the Jews from Spain.

The Hebrew version of *Bilawhar and Būdhāsaf* was composed by Abraham ibn Ḥasdāy some time before his death in 1240. Ibn Ḥasdāy was from Barcelona, at the time part of the kingdom of Aragon. He was an active translator of works from Arabic, as well as a philosopher. Medieval Jewish philosophy sought to reach the truth through human reason.[6] This may explain why Ibn Ḥasdāy was drawn to the story of a hermit who teaches a prince to use the powers of reason to understand God's truths.

It is not known which version of the Arabic *Bilawhar and Būdhāsaf* Ibn Ḥasdāy used for his adaptation, called *The Book of the Prince and the Hermit*.[7] The Hebrew text freely adapts *Bilawhar and Būdhāsaf* and includes only the prologue and the first part, that is, up to the departure of the hermit.[9] Some passages have been omitted—including the parable of the man in the well—and there are many additions, including new parables. Ibn Ḥasdāy added citations from the Bible and the Talmud, as well as many sayings attributed to wise men, probably from Arabic sources. The plot itself is not greatly changed; it begins with the cruel and idolatrous king who wishes to isolate his son from knowledge of the sorrows of the world. In *The Prince and the Hermit*, the king sends his son to an isolated island, where the hermit joins him and teaches the prince to recognize the vanity of life. The son learns his lessons well and wishes only to be a prophet of God's word.

*The Prince and the Hermit* was a popular work in Jewish circles. It continued to be published in Hebrew and was translated into Yiddish and German in the eighteenth and nineteenth centuries. It is yet another branch of the story, traveling to Europe not through Palestine but through North Africa. Rather than being adapted by Christians in Palestine, to be later translated into Latin and the vernaculars of Europe, Muslims carried the Arabic story across the straits of Gibraltar from North Africa to Europe. And there, in Muslim Spain, it was translated into Hebrew and adapted to Judaic culture.

Yet whether Jewish or Christian, the origins of the edifying legend of the prince who learns about God from a hermit had long been lost in time. The resemblance between the story of the prince and the story of the Buddha would continue to go unnoticed.

# CHAPTER SIX

# The Buddha Becomes Josaphat: Early Modern Readers

It seems unlikely that Marco Polo knew the story of Josaphat; Italian translations of the legend mostly postdate his departure from Venice in 1271.[1] He therefore would probably not have noticed the resemblance between the life story of Josaphat and the one that he recorded of Sagamoni Borcan (the Buddha). But one of his readers did. As we noted in our introduction, a fifteenth-century Italian scribe copying Marco Polo's book added the following note to his account of the life of the Buddha: "This is like the life of Saint Iosofat who was the son of the King Avenir of those parts of India, and was converted to the Christian faith by Barlaam, as it is read in the life and legend of the holy fathers."[2] This scribe could have known Italian translations of *Barlaam and Josaphat*, or, perhaps more likely, he could have known their story from the *Golden Legend*.

The compilation of saints' lives in the *Golden Legend* contributed to the popularity of Barlaam and Josaphat, and their status was further solidified when they were assigned a feast day (November 27). It is not clear when Barlaam and Josaphat first entered the church's record of saints, but they are present in the *Catalogus Sanctorum* by Petrus Natalibus, Bishop of Equilio, completed near the end of the fourteenth century. Pope Sixtus V authorized Cardinal Cesare Baronius (1538– 1607) to create a standard *martyrologium*, or martyrology, for the Roman Catholic Church, entitled *Tractatio de Martyrologio Romano*. In this work of prodigious scholarship, published in 1586, one finds for November 27, "Among the Indians, near the Persian boundary, the Saints Barlaam and Josaphat, whose wondrous deeds were written by St. John of Damascus."[3]

## Barlaam and Josaphat Enter History

If scholars and theologians had questions about the authenticity of saints Barlaam and Josaphat as the *Martyrology* was reprinted and reread over the centuries, any doubts about the story would have been based on the narrative itself, which may have seemed more story than history. For a seventeenth-century reader, for example, "Although its realism is accurate, it has many of the characteristics of fiction. . . . However, I do not wish to claim that the story is entirely invented; it would be rash to claim that there had never been a Barlaam or Josaphat. Since the *Roman Martyrology* includes them among the saints, there is no room for doubt."[4] An eighteenth-century edition of the *Martyrology* qualifies the entry on Saints Barlaam and Josaphat with the marginal note: "we do not know the date of their death or even if the story is only an allegory."[5]

In the following century, the connection of Josaphat to the

Buddha would become the subject of scholarly inquiry and the "wondrous deeds" of conversion that earned sainthood for Barlaam and Josaphat would be called into question. Noting that doubts had been raised about the historicity of Barlaam and Josaphat for centuries, the Roman Catholic scholar Emmanuel Cosquin (1841–1919) defended changes in the lists of recognized saints that were made as historical evidence was uncovered. He noted that in previous centuries scholars had expressed doubts based only on an examination of the legend itself. If they had been able to see documents that refuted its historicity, "their last hesitations would have fallen."[6] Yet although Cosquin insisted that Barlaam and Josaphat did not belong in Catholic martyrologies, he ardently defended the infallibility of the pope and the papal process of canonization, emphasizing that the printed record of saints was not produced by the pope himself and that there was a long tradition of corrections to the *Martyrology*.[7] Nonetheless, Barlaam and Josaphat maintained their saints' day in the martyrology of 1900, long after Josaphat's true identity had been revealed.

Barlaam and Josaphat finally lost their place in the catalog of Catholic saints, in part because no authoritative source testified to the truth of their lives. Their demotion from sanctity was surely also motivated by the growing understanding of the resemblance of Josaphat's life to the life of the Buddha and an uneasiness about the possibility that the story of a Christian saint famed for his condemnation of idolatry and for his conversion of India to Christianity was in fact based on the story of a pagan from India, a land that had never been converted. As we shall see below, one of the several ironies in the text is that for centuries Christians regarded the Buddha, the figure upon whom Josaphat is based, as an idol, and Buddhism as idolatry.

## The Buddha as Idol

In describing Sagamoni Borcan, Marco Polo wrote, "And they do hold him for the greatest of all their gods. And they tell that the aforesaid image of him was the first idol that the Idolaters ever had; and from that have originated all the other idols." We cringe today at the identification of Buddhists as "idolaters," but there were few terms available to Marco Polo for foreigners who seem to worship statues. We might wonder how he would have described Christian devotion to statues of the Virgin Mary had he cast his ethnographic gaze on his own countrymen. For many medieval writers all pagans were idolaters, and even Muslims, who forbid any representation of God, are described as idolaters in many medieval texts. It is not surprising then that Marco Polo would describe Buddhists as idolaters. Indeed, until well into the nineteenth century Europeans typically divided the peoples of the world into four nations: Christians, Jews, Muslims (often called "Mahometans"), and Idolaters or Pagans. Buddhists fell into this last large category. According to the *Oxford English Dictionary*, the term Buddhism (spelled "Boudhism") did not even appear in English until 1801.

When Marco Polo says that the Buddha was "the first idol the Idolaters ever had," he is not claiming that idols of the Buddha were made before the children of Israel made the golden calf at Sinai. He is not referring to a biblical story but to a Buddhist story he heard in China. During the first century CE, it is said that the emperor Ming had a dream about a golden man flying with rays of light emanating from his head. He reported the dream to his ministers, who informed him that the golden man was the Buddha, a sage from the West. The emperor sent a delegation to retrieve his teachings and, according to one version of the story, they returned with a text and a statue. This was how Buddhism came to China, and the statue became the model for all future images of the Buddha. Hence, Marco Polo says, "the aforesaid image of him was the first idol that the Idolaters ever had; and from that have originated all the other idols."

European travelers would encounter many statues of the Buddha in the centuries that followed. Each Buddhist culture has its own artistic conventions and styles of representing the Buddha, and each Buddhist culture has a different name for the Buddha in its local languages. He is Fo and Shijiamouni in Chinese, Shaka and Hotoke in Japanese, Sommona Codom in Thai, Sang-gye and Shakya-thupba in Tibetan, and, as above, Sagamoni Borcan in Mongolian.

As Christian missionaries made their way to Asia, first to the courts of the Mongol khans beginning in the late thirteenth century and then to India, Sri Lanka, Japan, Tibet, and Southeast Asia, the supposed idolatry of the Buddhists became an urgent concern: the idolaters had to be converted. In the sixteenth century, Matteo Ricci, an Italian Jesuit missionary to China, would argue, in Chinese, that the golden man of the emperor's dream was in fact Jesus and that the delegation the emperor sent to learn about him was supposed to have gone farther west, all the way to Palestine, to retrieve the Gospels. Ricci's own mission was then the true fulfillment of the emperor's wishes.

The Buddha, known by many names, would be excoriated as an idol and a sinister purveyor of idolatry by numerous Christian writers over several centuries. One was Francis Xavier, who arrived in Japan with three of his fellow Jesuit priests and a Japanese translator on July 27, 1549, roughly a generation before Matteo Ricci was sent to China. He had gone to Japan thinking that the Japanese believed in God and that he would find fellow Christians there. He was disappointed when he found out he was wrong:

> I tried to learn if these two, Ameda [Amitābha] and Xaca [Śākyamuni], had been men dedicated to philosophy. I asked the Christians to make an accurate translation of their lives. I discovered from what was written in their books that they were not men, since it was written that they had lived for a thousand and two thousand years, and that Xaca will be born eight thousand times, and many other absurdities. They were thus not men, but pure inventions of the demons.
>
> For the love and service of our Lord, I entreat all those who will read this letter to ask God to give us victory over these two demons, Xaca and Ameda, and over all the others as well, for in the city of Yamaguchi, through the goodness of God, they are already losing the credit which they used to have.[8]

Although they found no Christians, the Jesuits established a mission in Japan that had some success. In 1590, they brought a movable-type printing press to Japan. The earliest of the surviving books from their printing efforts was *Sanctos no Gosagveono Vchinvqigaqi* (*Compendium of the Acts of the Saints*), published in 1591. It contained a full translation of *Barlaam and Josaphat* into Japanese (written in Roman characters). And so this story with scenes from the life of the Buddha that would have been familiar to the Japanese was brought to a Buddhist land to convert the idolaters to Christianity. The story may have seemed all the more appropriate because just four years earlier, the shogun Toyotomi Hideyoshi had issued a ban on Christianity, taking on the role of a latter-day King Avenir.[9]

Knowledge about Asia and the practices of Buddhism came from missionaries, though they sometimes distorted it beyond recognition in their descriptions. Other learned Europeans also wrote about Asia, offering descriptions of its religion often without ever leaving Europe. One of the most famous of these was the Jesuit savant Athanasius Kircher (1602–1680), described as "the last man who knew everything." He wrote some forty works on a remarkable range of topics, including *China Illustrata*, published in Latin in 1667. Kircher drew from the large corpus of reports and letters sent back to Rome by his fellow Jesuits on missions in India, Tibet, China, and Japan to postulate that the idolatry found in China had originated in Egypt. He notes that in 525 BCE, the Persian king Cambyses II, son of Cyrus the Great, defeated the Egyptians at the Battle of Pelusium. Herodotus reports that the Persians advanced into battle carrying cats, knowing that the Egyptians would not shoot their arrows for fear of harming their sacred animal. Cambyses then led his army to Memphis, where he captured the pharaoh and put hundreds of his priests to the sword. Kircher explains that some of the Egyptian priests escaped by sea to India, where they promulgated the worship of Egyptian gods. From there, Egyptian religion, including the doctrine of the transmigration of souls, spread to Indochina, China, and Japan.

Kircher calls Buddhism the sect of Siequa (that is, Śākyamuni Buddha), saying of Buddhists, "When we investigate this sect, its doctrines show that it came from the naked philosophers of the brahmins, Persians, and Bactrians, who formerly inhabited all Indostan. They believe in a multitude of worlds and in metempsychosis, which is the entrance of human souls into animals, and in all the Pythagorean teachings. . . . They live apart on hills and in caves for the sake of meditation. Their temples are full of huge idols of bronze, marble, wood, and clay. You would think these are Egyptian shrines."[10] The figure blamed for spreading Egyptian superstition across Asia was the Buddha, who, among other heresies, taught reincarnation, a doctrine that European scholars of the day associated with Pythagoras. Kircher provided the following account of his life:

The first creator and architect of the superstition was a very sinful brahmin imbued with Pythagoreanism. He was not content just to spread the doctrine, but even added to it so much that there is scarcely any one who is able to describe the doctrine or to write about it. He was an imposter known all over the East. The Indians called him Rama, the Chinese Xe Kian, the Japanese Xaca, and the Turks Chiaga. This deadly monster was born in central India in the place which the Chinese call Tien Truc Gnoc. His birth was portentous. They say his mother had a dream and saw a white elephant come first from her mouth and then from her left side. . . . So Xaca was born and he was the first who is said to have killed his mother. Then he pointed one hand toward heaven and the other down to the earth and said that except for him, there was none holy, not in heaven nor in earth. Then he betook himself to the mountain recesses and there he instituted this abominable idolatry with Satan's help. Afterwards he infected the whole Orient with his pestilent dogmas. The Chinese Annals say that when he emerged from his solitary hermitage, a divine (or more likely, a satanic) spirit filled him. He gathered together about 80,000 disciples. He selected 500 of these, and then 100 from these. Finally, he selected ten as being the best suited for teaching his horrible doctrines. He had chosen them as intimate counselors and associates in his crimes. Lest his doctrines be called in question by anyone, when dying, he decreed that the Pythagorean epithet be placed in his books. This phrase is, "He himself said," or, "So our books teach us." This means that it is evil to question the truth or the infallibility of these absurd fables, which are horrible and execrable. These are not tenets, but crimes. They are not doctrines, but abominations. They are not histories, but fables.[11]

We find a similarly negative view of the Buddha in the writings of Louis le Comte (1655–1728), a French Jesuit missionary to Siam (Thailand) and China and one of the six Jesuit scientists who accompanied the first French delegation to the Court of Siam, sent by Louis XIV in 1685. Five of the priests, including le Comte, continued on to China, arriving in 1688. Upon his return to France, he published his *Nouveaux mémoires sur l'état présent de la Chine* in 1696. In the passage below, which begins with an allusion to the emperor Ming's embrace of Buddhism, he refers to the Buddha as the god Fo, the Chinese word for Buddha.

This Poyson began at Court, but spread its infection thro' all the Provinces, and corrupted every Town: so that this great body of Men already spoiled by Magick and Impiety, was immediately infected with Idolatry, and became a monstrous receptacle for all sorts of Errors. Fables, Superstitions, Transmigration of Souls, Idolatry and Atheism divided them, and got so strong a Mastery over them, that, even at this present, there is no so great impediment to the progress of Christianity as is this ridiculous and impious Doctrine. . . .

Thus the Devil making use of Men's Folly and Malice for their destruction, endeavours to erase out of the minds of some those excellent ideas of God which are so deeply ingraved there, and to imprint in the minds of others the Worship of false Gods under the shapes of a multitude of different Creatures, for they did not stop at the Worship of this Idol. The Ape, the Elephant, the

Dragon have been worshipped in several places, under pretense perhaps that the God *Fo* had successively been transmigrated into these Creatures. *China* the most superstitious of all Nations, increased the Number of her Idols, and one may now see all sorts of them in the Temples, which serve to abuse the folly of this People.[12]

For centuries, Europeans regarded images of the Buddha across Asia as idols of different deities. It was only at the end of the seventeenth century that it came to be understood that they represented the same figure, although known by different names. Over the course of the eighteenth century, it came to be generally accepted that the Buddha was a historical figure, although his place of birth remained a point of contention; some claimed that he came from Egypt.

Because the life story of the Buddha had been known in Europe for some centuries, albeit generally in the negative forms described in the Jesuit accounts above, it seems surprising that the connection between the Buddha and Josaphat would become a point of scholarly interest only in the last half of the nineteenth century. In fact, the connection had been made some three centuries before, in 1612, by the Portuguese soldier and chronicler Diogo de Couto (1542–1616):

To this name [the Buddha] the Gentiles throughout all India have dedicated great and superb pagodas. With reference to this story we have been diligent in enquiring if the ancient Gentiles of those parts had in their writing any knowledge of St. Josaphat who was con-

verted by Barlão, who in his Legend is represented as
the son a great King of India, and who had just the same
up-bringing, with all the same particulars, that we have
recounted of the life of Budão. And since the story of
Josaphat was written by the natives during his time (and
nothing else was left for them to write), it appears that
over time they added many fables, like those from the
life of Budão, which we are going to leave, because it
would take more than two chapters to tell them in the
way they do.

And as a thing seems much to the purpose, which
was told to us by a very old man of Salsette territory in
Baçaim, about Josaphat, and it seems appropriate to cite
it: As I was travelling in the Isle of Salsette, and went
to see that rare and admirable Pagoda (which they call
Canará Pagoda) made in a mountain, with many halls cut
out of solid rock, and one of them is as large as the great
hall of the Ribeira Palace in Lisbon. There are more than
three hundred chambers reaching up to the summit, laid
out like a spiral, each chamber having its own cistern at
the door, and the cistern is carved in the same stone and
it gives the coldest and most excellent water you could
wish for. At the door of the great hall there are magnif-
icent stone statues as large as giants; they are made in a
delicate and splendid manner that could not be matched
even in silver; there were other wonderful things that I
will not describe in order to avoid being long-winded.

Enquiring from this old man about the work, and
what he thought as to who made it, he told us that with-

out doubt the work was made by order of the father of
St. Josaphat to bring him up therein in seclusion, as the
story tells. And as it informs us that he was the son of
a great King of India, it may well be, as we have just
said, that *he* was the Budão, of whom they relate such
marvels.[13]

This is an important passage and worthy of comment. We
should begin with the geographical references. De Couto spent
much of his life in India, departing for his first trip in 1557, when
he was fifteen years old. He traveled widely, spending the last
years of his life in Goa on the western coast, at the time a Portuguese colony. In the passage above, he mentions the "Salsette territory in Baçaim." Baçaim (also known as Bassein) was
a Portuguese fortress-town on the Indian Ocean. At the time
of de Couto, it ruled a significant region that extended south to
include Salsette Island, the site of modern Mumbai (Bombay).
On the island, there is a famous Buddhist cave-temple com-
plex called Kanheri (Canará above), with more than a hundred
caves and dating from between the first century and the tenth
century CE.

De Couto describes the caves in grand terms, comparing
the great hall of one of them to the royal palace in Lisbon
(which would be destroyed in the great earthquake and tsu-
nami of 1755). What makes this passage particularly interest-
ing for our story is that he reports that an old man told him
that this was the palace that King Avenir had built for Prince
Josaphat to shield him from the sorrows of the world.

We can conclude that at the end of the sixteenth century,

this learned European historian regarded Josaphat and his father as historical figures and *Barlaam and Josaphat* as a historical account of Barlaam's conversion of Josaphat, who then went on to convert all of India to Christianity. Later in his account de Couto describes a footprint in stone that he saw in India and which he believes is that of Saint Thomas. For de Couto, India had once been Christian, converted most recently by Josaphat.

We see here another example of the dream of conversion. Europeans of previous centuries believed that the apostle Thomas spread the Gospel in India and converted Indian kings. During the time of the Crusades, Christians hoped for the arrival of Prester John, a Christian king who was believed to have converted the East. Here, we see that some version of the life of the Buddha reminds de Couto of the life of Josaphat. And he goes further, imagining that the Buddha was in fact a corrupted version of Josaphat, and that over the centuries, Christianity had died out and the true story of Josaphat, the prince who had converted India to Christianity, had become mixed with fables about a wise man whom the Gentiles, that is, the idolaters, called Budão. But in fact, the Buddha and Josaphat were the same.

In the period between the sixteenth and nineteenth centuries, the fame of *Barlaam and Josaphat* largely faded, although it could be used by Catholics against their rivals. In 1577 and 1578, the Abbé de Billy published new translations of the tale from Greek into Latin and from Latin into French, explaining, "We print, we adapt the *Barlaam* because it is a serious weapon against Luther and the innovators, it exalts and justifies Christian monasticism."[14] The other occasional references from this period deal not with the story's sources but with its authenticity: is the tale history or fable? If it is fable, were Barlaam and Josaphat nonetheless historical figures? During that same period, the Buddha remained an idol, with similar questions raised about whether he was a historical person.

De Couto's connection of Josaphat and the Buddha would be ignored or misunderstood for centuries. François Valentijn (1666–1727) was a clergyman who served in the Dutch East India Company as a pastor and missionary in what is today Indonesia. Upon his return to the Netherlands, he wrote a five-volume history of the Dutch East India Company and the lands visited by its officers. In the course of his research on Sri Lanka for *Old and New East Indies* (*Oud en Nieuw Oost-Indiën*), published between 1724 and 1726, Valentijn came across the passage from Diogo de Couto. However, because he seems never to have heard of Josaphat, he misunderstood it. He wrote, "There be some who hold this Budhum for a fugitive Syrian Jew, or for an Israelite, others who hold him for a Disciple of the Apostle Thomas; but how in that case he could have been born 622 years before Christ I leave them to explain. Diego de Couto stands by the belief that he was certainly *Joshua*, which is still more absurd!"[15]

De Couto would be given his due only in the nineteenth century, in a densely annotated translation of the travels of Marco Polo, *The Book of Ser Marco Polo the Venetian Concerning the Kingdoms and Marvels of the East*, published by the Scottish Orientalist and veteran of the Sikh Wars Henry Yule (1820–1889) in 1871. Yule provides a footnote about the life of the Buddha, augmented substantially in the second edition of 1875, with a discussion of *Barlaam and Josaphat*. Yule's elaboration of the similarities between the stories of the Christian saint and the Buddha is a mark of his exceptional scholarship; it is also a sign that the European perception of the Buddha had changed. By the time that Yule published his translation, European scholars had learned to read the languages of Buddhism.

# CHAPTER SEVEN

# Josaphat Becomes the Buddha:
# Modern Readers

During what used to be called the Age of Discovery (the centuries during which European mariners "discovered" the Americas and Asia) and continuing into what is still called the Age of Colonialism (when European powers brought large regions of those continents under their rule), the Buddha was an idol to be condemned and Buddhists were idolaters to be converted. The elements of the life of the Buddha in the story of Barlaam and Josaphat went largely unnoticed; they were simply scenes in this tale known above all for its parables. For the very few who noted a similarity, the Buddha looked like Josaphat. It was only in the nineteenth century that Josaphat began to look like the Buddha. But this could only happen when the Buddha turned from an idol carved in stone to a sage of flesh and blood.

It is perhaps not surprising that the European view of the Buddha began to change when the British East India Company gained control of India. Buddhism had largely disappeared from India by the fourteenth century. The European travelers who encountered Buddhism in China, Japan, Tibet, Siam, Ceylon, and Burma saw monks and nuns in active monasteries and temples, but travelers to India found only the ruins of Buddhism: deserted cave monasteries, indecipherable inscriptions, crumbling reliquaries, and stone statues, sometime headless, of the Buddha. In 1786, Sir William Jones, a judge at the Calcutta court, famously declared that there was a linguistic affinity between the classical Indian language Sanskrit and Greek and Latin. The work of Jones and other officers of the East India Company created a kind of Sanskrit craze in Europe, with the first chair in Sanskrit established at the Collège de France in 1814. Friedrich Schelling declared the dawn of a new Renaissance, this one based not on the recovery of the classics of Greece and Rome but on the recovery of the classics of India. The Buddha would play a major role.

During the first decades of the nineteenth century, there were a small number of Europeans with sufficient skill in various Asian languages to produce accurate translations of Buddhist texts. No Sanskrit texts had been discovered; the first translations of Buddhist scriptures were made from Tibetan, Chinese, and Mongolian. There were many Hindu Sanskrit texts, and from them—and from the Brahmins with whom the British worked so closely in their translations—the British learned that the Buddha had criticized the caste system and had condemned animal sacrifice, two things that appealed to the sensibility of late eighteenth-century Europe. The British concluded, wrongly, that the reason Buddhism no longer existed in India was because the egalitarian Buddhists had been driven out by the narrow-minded Brahmins.

In 1821, Brian Houghton Hodgson, a young officer of the East India Company posted in Nepal (where Buddhism had survived), learned of the existence of Buddhist Sanskrit texts in Kathmandu. Over the next two decades, he acquired copies of dozens of these works and shipped them to the Company's headquarters in Calcutta, and to London, Oxford, and Paris. The first shipment to Paris arrived in 1837, where they were read by a young scholar named Eugène Burnouf (1801–1852), who five years earlier had been appointed to the Sanskrit chair at the Collège de France. Burnouf was the son of a distinguished classicist and had studied Sanskrit with his father as a boy. In his diary entry of March 20, 1845, his student Friedrich Max Müller (who would go on to become the most famous Orientalist of the century) described his first meeting with his future teacher: "Went to see Burnouf. Spiritual, amiable, thoroughly French. He received me in the most friendly way, talked a great deal, and all he said was valuable, not on ordinary topics but on special. I managed better in French than I expected. 'I am a Brahman, a Buddhist, a Zoroastrian. I hate the Jesuits'—that is the sort of man. I am looking forward to his lectures."[1]

The Sanskrit manuscripts Burnouf received from Hodgson included many of the most important texts in the history of Buddhism, including the *Lotus Sūtra*, which Burnouf would translate in full. However, he felt that a European audience would not understand the translation without some background, and so prior to its publication, he wrote *Introduction à l'histoire du*

*Buddhisme indien*, a work with a modest title that would prove to be the most influential book on Buddhism in the nineteenth century. It was 647 pages in length, and Burnouf intended it as only the first of as many as four volumes; he did not live to complete the others.

In the various Sanskrit manuscripts from Nepal, Burnouf discerned the historical evolution of Buddhism. It began with the Buddha himself in works that Burnouf called "the simple sūtras." These were the works that Burnouf felt most closely reflected the Buddha's own teachings. Other texts were filled with miracles and metaphysics. For Burnouf, these works, which he called "the developed sūtras," were from a later period, long after the Buddha's death. Burnouf's clear preference was for the earlier ones. "The ordinary sūtras show us Śākyamuni Buddha preaching his doctrine in the midst of a society that, judging from the legends in which he plays a role, was profoundly corrupt. His teaching is above all moral; and although metaphysics are not forgotten, it certainly occupies a less grand position than the theory of virtues imposed by the law of the Buddha, virtues among which charity, patience, and chastity are without objection at the first rank."[2] Burnouf calls this "human Buddhism," and he regards it as the most ancient and the most authentic.

For Burnouf, the Buddha was a pivotal figure in Indian history, indeed bringing Indian religion (although he hesitates to even call the Buddhism of the Buddha a religion, seeing it instead as a philosophy) down from the flights of mystical fancy to the real world of human suffering. "He lived, he taught, and he died as a philosopher; and his humanity remained a fact so incontestably recognized by all that the compilers of legends to whom miracles cost so little did not even have the thought of making him a god after his death."[3]

Burnouf makes no mention of Christianity in his *Introduction*, but in the decades after his death, his readers would draw the connection between the teacher from India and the teacher from Palestine. As Hermann Oldenberg wrote in his *Buddha, His Life, His Doctrine, His Order* in 1881, "An itinerant teacher and his itinerant followers, not unlike those bands, who in later times bore through Galilee the tidings: 'the kingdom of heaven is at hand,' went through the realms of India with the burden of sorrow and death, and the announcement, 'open ye your ears; the deliverance from death is found.'"[4]

Others would note how the Buddha's ethical teachings, as they moved beyond the borders of his native India, had been polluted by magic and superstition, even having their own pope, as some called the mysterious high lama of Tibet. For some Protestant scholars, the parallels between the Buddhism of the Buddha in ancient India and the Buddhism Europeans encountered in modern Asia, and "primitive Christianity" (as the teachings of Jesus were called) and the Roman Catholic Church were clear. Soon, some were calling the Buddha, "the Luther of Asia."

One of the implications of this particular portrait of the Buddha was that true Buddhism, original Buddhism, primitive Buddhism, was long dead, no longer to be found among the millions of Buddhists across Asia. Instead, it was to be found in Sanskrit and Pali texts—texts best understood not in Asia but in the libraries of Europe. With the links between classical

Sanskrit and Greek and Latin, the Buddha's affinities seemed somehow closer to ancient Europe than modern Asia. These bonds grew stronger with the rise of the science of philology, which identified Greek, Latin, Sanskrit, German, English, and French as "Aryan languages," different in fundamental ways from the Semitic languages of Hebrew and Arabic and the Turanian languages of Chinese, Japanese, and Mongolian. Even the original language of the Buddhist scriptures shared more in common with Greek and Latin than with Chinese and Japanese. As race theory developed, the Aryan language family would become a bloodline. Here again, the Buddha was related to Europeans as Jews and Muslims were not.

Thus, in the first list of the "world religions" (*Weltreligionen*) there were only two, Christianity and Buddhism. They were said to warrant this title because each had a universal message, and because that message had spread around the world through the power of its truth rather than by the power of the sword (as Islam had). Each had grown from a local religion (*Landesreligion*)—Judaism for Christianity and Hinduism for Buddhism—religions that were bound by their ethnicity from spreading from their native place, except when forced to do so by diaspora. Both Buddhism and Christianity were religions with a single founder and a single savior who had rejected a benighted priesthood that would condemn him.

Where there was kinship there was also antithesis. Christianity and Buddhism became mirror images of each other; one a religion of the West, the other of the East; one theistic, the other atheistic; one with a reluctant savior, the other with a savior who proclaimed his superiority from the moment of his birth; one whose savior is depicted nailed to a cross, the other whose savior is depicted seated cross-legged in meditation.

And so the Buddha became something of a cultural hero in Victorian Europe, especially in certain learned and liberal circles. In 1879, Edwin Arnold published his verse version of the life of the Buddha, which he entitled *The Light of Asia*. It was a bestseller and a favorite of Queen Victoria, and at the death of Tennyson, Arnold was among those considered for Poet Laureate. We should note that Arnold's work did not enjoy universal acclaim and was attacked by a number of Christian clergy, leading him to make amends in 1891 with *The Light of the World*, a telling of the life of Jesus. It was not a bestseller.

In some of the more eccentric corners of European scholarship, the parallels between primitive Buddhism and primitive Christianity, between the Buddha and Christ, were not enough; for some, Jesus was a Buddhist. We find such works as *Buddhism in Christendom: Or, Jesus, the Essene* (1887) and *The Influence of Buddhism on Primitive Christianity* (1893) by Arthur Lillie, and *The Angel Messiah of Buddhists, Essenes, and Christian* (1880) by Ernest De Bunsen. The Russian aristocrat Nicola Notovitch claimed to find in Ladakh a text called *The Life of Saint Issa* that proved Jesus had spent his "lost years" (between the ages of twelve and thirty, undocumented in the Gospels) in India, where he became a Buddhist. The eccentricity of such works was not always benign; in the days of high race theory, they were among the many attempts to separate Jesus from Judaism.

Perhaps the Buddha could not be identified with Josaphat prior to the nineteenth century because the Buddha was an idol and Josaphat was a saint. In the Roman Catholic rhetoric about the Buddha, praise of his life and deeds is rare; as we have seen, he is almost universally demonized as an idol and purveyor of idolatry. This makes Marco Polo's statement all the more striking: "If he had been a Christian, he would have been a great saint of Our Lord Jesus Christ, so good and pure was the life he led." But even here, there is a hint of converting him to Christianity, with sanctity to be found only in the Christian church. All of this would change in the nineteenth and twentieth centuries. In the process, Josaphat would lose his sainthood and the Buddha would become a saint of a more catholic church. The nineteenth-century rediscovery of the Buddhist influence on *Barlaam and Josaphat* created something of a sensation, generating both delight and dismay.

## Saint Buddha

The first scholar to notice a connection between *Barlaam and Josaphat* and ancient India appears to have been the eminent scholar of Sanskrit Theodor Benfey (1809–1881), who noted it in the introduction to his two-volume translation of the *Pañcatantra*, a famous collection of Indian fables, published in Leipzig in 1853.[5] Benfey was able to trace one of the most famous parables in *Barlaam and Josaphat*, the parable of the man in the well, to the *Pañcatantra*. The French savant Édouard Laboulaye (1811–1883), best remembered for his books on American politics and law, was the first to draw a direct parallel between the life of Josaphat and the life of the Buddha. He did so in an article in the July 26, 1859, issue of the weekly newspaper *Jour-*

*nal des débats politiques et littéraires.* He locates the resemblance
in the story of the chariot rides. After describing them briefly,
he writes, "This story is so characteristic and the encounters
so distinctive, it is the very same as the romance of Josaphat.
Such similarities are not caused by chance; we must recognize
the Orient at work here."[6] In the following year, the German
folklorist and translator of *Barlaam and Josaphat*, Felix Liebrecht (1812–1890), published an article linking the story to a
specific Buddhist text, the famously baroque life of the Buddha
called the *Lalitavistara*.[7] Liebrecht was in fact mistaken in his
association, likely made because the *Lalitavistara* was the only
biography of the Buddha that had been translated into a European language at that time; the French scholar of Sanskrit and
Tibetan Philippe Édouard Foucaux (1811–1894), a student of
Burnouf, had translated the text from the Tibetan in 1847.[8]

In a lecture entitled, "On the Migration of Fables" delivered at the Royal Institution in London on June 3, 1870, Friedrich Max Müller, who became the most famous scholar of
Asian religions of the nineteenth century, discussed *Barlaam
and Josaphat* at some length, arguing in favor of the ascrip-
tion of the Greek text to John of Damascus, stating that "the
early life of Josaphat is exactly the same as that of Buddha."
As we recall, in the prologue to the Greek version of the story,
the unnamed narrator describes it as "the edifying story that
has come to me, delivered by devout men from the inner land
of the Ethiopians, whom our tale calls Indians, and translated
from trustworthy records." Müller accepted this as a statement
of fact and took it a step further: "one might almost believe that
Joannes Damascenus [John of Damascus] did not only hear

the story of Buddha, as he says, from the mouth of people who had brought it to him from India, but that he had before him the very text of the *Lalita Vistara*."[9] Müller was wrong about John of Damascus and wrong about the *Lalitavistara*. Still, his final comments capture why the claim to sameness—and more specifically, that Josaphat looked like the Buddha—would captivate so many:

If, then, Joannes Damascenus tells the same story, only putting the name of Joasaph or Josaphat, *i.e.*, Bodhi-sattva, in the place of Buddha; if all that is human and personal in the life of St. Josaphat is taken from the 'Lalita Vistara'—what follows? It follows that . . . St. Josaphat is the Buddha of the Buddhist canon. It follows that Buddha has become a saint in the Roman Church; it follows that, though under a different name, the sage of Kapilavastu, the founder of a religion which, whatever we may think of its dogma, is, in the purity of its morals, nearer to Christianity than any other religion, and which counts even now, after an existence of 2,400 years, 455,000,000 of believers, has received the highest honors that the Christian Church can bestow. And whatever we may think of the sanctity of saints, let those who doubt the right of Buddha to a place among them read the story of his life as it is told in the Buddhist canon. If he lived the life which is there described, few saints have a better claim to the title than Buddha; and no one either in the Greek or in the Roman Church need be ashamed of having paid to the Buddha's memory the

honor that was intended for St. Josaphat the prince, the
hermit, and the saint.

History, here as elsewhere, is stranger than fiction;
and a kind fairy, whom men call Chance, has here, as
elsewhere, remedied the ingratitude and injustice of the
world.[10]

It is not exactly clear what Müller means by the last sentence. Perhaps he sees the Buddha, so long excoriated as an
idol, finally recognized for who he is: the spiritual equal of any
Christian saint. An injustice has been righted, and a different
kind of conversion had occurred. The Buddha had become a
saint, and a Christian saint, Josaphat, had become the Buddha. But the Buddha had become a saint not by the sanction
of the Catholic Church, which had condemned him as an
idol for so long, but because he was holy. He was a saint of a
human religion whose foundations were the "charity, patience,
and chastity" that Müller's teacher Burnouf had described a
quarter-century before, foundations that were not the property of any single creed.

Müller's statement was quoted approvingly by the leading
British scholar of Buddhism of the day (and a former colonial
official in Sri Lanka), Thomas W. Rhys Davids in his 1880
*Buddhist Birth-Stories*, a study of the Buddhist *jātakas*, or stories of the Buddha's former lives. These stories, sometimes
referred to as a Buddhist version of *Aesop's Fables*, contain
Buddhist adaptations of well-known Indian tales. Rhys Davids
sets out to show the Indian and Buddhist origin of many of
the most famous European fables (including many of *Aesop's*

*Fables*), tracing their routes of transmission where possible. In the course of the discussion, he provides a lengthy section on *Barlaam and Josaphat*, claiming, like Müller, that the Buddha "appealed so strongly to the sympathies, and was so attractive to the minds of medieval Christians, that he became, and has ever since remained, an object of Christian worship."[11]

The changing fortunes of Josaphat and the Buddha in Europe are also evident in their treatment in the great encyclopedias of the day. Barlaam and Josaphat warranted their own entry ("Barlaam and Josaphat, Saints") in the ninth edition of the *Encyclopedia Britannica* published between 1875 and 1889. The entry, composed by Henry Yule, the translator of Marco Polo, begins by providing their saints' days in "the Greek and Roman Martyrology" and then announces that "their story is in the highest degree worthy of note, because it is, in fact, a Christianized version of the Indian legendary history of the Buddha, Sakya Muni." In the second paragraph, Yule notes that "many readers may be unaware that Sakya Muni himself, or as he was by birth, Siddharta [*sic*], the son of Suddodhana [*sic*], prince of Kapilavastu (in the north of modern Oudh), has found his way into the Roman calendar as a saint of the church." Later in the longish entry, he declares, although incorrectly, that, "Now this story is, in all essentials and in many details, *mutatis mutandis*, the story of Buddha." The entry in the 1911 edition of the *Encyclopedia Britannica* is essentially a paraphrase and updating of Yule's piece. However, the anonymous author confidently declares near the end, "Thus unwittingly Gautama the Buddha has come to official recognition as a saint in two great branches of the Catholic Church, and no one will say that he does not deserve the honour." The anti-Catholic tone that appears in so much British writing on *Barlaam and Josaphat* from this period is evident here; the Roman Catholic Church had been regarded with suspicion in England since the time of Henry VIII. This did not mean that the scholars of the colonial period objected to missions to convert the Buddhists of Asia to Protestant Christianity. As we have noted above, Burnouf's creation of the human Buddha allowed Europeans to separate the ancient Buddha from modern Buddhists, to exalt the first for his teachings and demean the second for corrupting those teachings.

One of the most authoritative reference works in the field of religion during the first half of the twentieth century was the twelve-volume *Encyclopedia of Religion and Ethics*, edited by the Scottish biblical scholar James Hastings (1852–1922) and published between 1908 and 1926 with contributions from many of the greatest scholars of the day. (Affectionately known often simply as "Hastings," the spine of its final volume memorably reads, "Suffering to Zwingli.") Here, one finds Barlaam and Josaphat by a circuitous route. The entry for Barlaam in the second volume (which covers "Arthur" to "Bunyan") provides the instruction, "See Buddha." Yet one reads the long and learned entry by Alfred Shenington Geden (1857–1936) in vain, finding no mention of Barlaam whatsoever until the end, where a notice in brackets reads: "The subject of Barlaam and Josaphat, which was referred to this article by cross-reference at BARLAAM, it has been found more convenient to treat in a separate article under the title JOSAPHAT." In the seventh volume ("Hymns" to "Liberty"), we eventually find a lengthy entry, again by the same author. Geden was an Orientalist in the original sense of the term, writing on the Hebrew Bible, the Greek New Testament, and comparative religion more broadly, and his focus is very much the textual history of the story.

## The Quest for the Source

In the last half of the nineteenth century, much scholarly attention was thus devoted to *Barlaam and Josaphat*, and many versions would be published, translated from a variety of languages. In some cases, the authors devoted their attention to matters of philology. In others, however, they pondered larger questions. Here we might consider two authors who had very different views of the same story.

In Calcutta in 1895, K. S. MacDonald, the British missionary to India and editor of the *Indian Evangelical Review*, published *The Story of Barlaam and Joasaph: Buddhism & Christianity*. In the preface, he explains that he found an English version of the story from 1732 in the British Library and decided that it would make an ideal reading assignment for Indian students at Calcutta University in a class on the development of the English language from the earliest times through the fourteenth century. One can certainly understand why the work would have appealed to MacDonald: it is an English story set in India in which the entire population of the subcontinent is converted from idolatry to Christianity. He devotes the introduction to the "endeavour to show that we have no reason to believe that either the Life of Buddha or the teaching or doctrine of Buddhism had any influence on the Gospels or other Scriptures of the New Testament—nay, more, that we have no reason to believe that the apostles of Christ, the writers of the New Testament, had ever heard of Buddha or of Buddhism."[12]

The following year, the distinguished Australian historian and folklorist Joseph Jacobs published in London *Barlaam and Josaphat: English Lives of Buddha*. He begins by confessing that the English versions of the story are "but poor things," and that he has collected them in this volume in order to write the introduction that follows. That introduction, almost one hundred pages long, begins and ends with remarkable pronouncements. It begins, "Buddha and Christ, it may be said, represent the two highest planes which the religious consciousness of mankind has hitherto reached. Each in his way represents the Ideal of a whole Continent. The aim of Asia has always been To Be, the aim of Europe, To Do. The contemplative Sage is the highest ideal of Asia. Europe pins its faith to the beneficent Saint."[13] This is a familiar cliché, which sadly persists to the present day—that "the West" is active and "the East" is passive, that the West is outward in its gaze and the East is inward.

Jacobs goes on to enumerate the many parallels in the lives of the two great founders that lead one to wonder whether Buddhism influenced Christianity. Unlike less circumspect scholars of the day, he defers this question in the case of Jesus himself "till Folklore has become so much of a Science as to be able to discriminate between foreign and independent origin." This leads him naturally to a consideration of the influence of Buddhism on *Barlaam and Josaphat*, which he considers in great detail, citing the by then considerable corpus of scholarship on the topic and drawing especially on the Prussian scholar Hermann Zotenberg (who posited the existence of a pre-Muslim version of the tale that originated in Persia and speculated that the figure of King Avenir may have been based on the sixth-century Persian monarch Khosrau I). Here and in an appendix, Jacobs provides a learned discussion of the major parables in the story, noting their appearance in a wide range of other sources. He speculates that there was a single Buddhist urtext (for which he even proposes a Sanskrit title, *Bhagavan Bodhisattvascha*) that included not only the legend of the Buddha but also most of the parables. This text was then translated into Persian during the reign of Khosrau I (whom he calls Chosroes) in the sixth century. The story became popular among the Muslims and Nestorian Christians of the region, who translated it into Arabic and Syriac. From Syriac, he claims, it made its way with various interpolations into the languages of Europe.

The passage that concludes Jacobs's introduction is perhaps even more striking than the one that begins it.

When we ask what is the charm which attracted mediaeval Christendom to what is, after all, only a version of the life and parables of Buddha, the answer is not far to seek. The world has known, up till now, four great systems of Religion: Paganism, Buddhism, Christianity, and Culture, of which last Goethe may be described as the High Priest. Paganism in its various forms may be most simply described as the Worship of the Social Bond. All the other three religions have for their main object the salvation of the individual. And all three are at one as to the means of salvation. "*Entbehren, entbehren sollst du,*" cried Goethe, and in his own way was only repeating what Buddha and Christ had said before him. Renunciation as the key of salvation is thus the teaching of all modern religions. It is because the Barlaam Legend, and many of its Parables, have presented renunciation as the ideal of man's striving, that it came home in the Middle Ages so persistently to the folk with whom renunciation is a necessity of existence. The truth embodied in this tale has indeed come home to lowly minds.[14]

Like the opening passage, this is a remarkable statement in many ways. As we have noted, prior to the nineteenth century, Europeans divided the peoples of the world into four nations: Christians, Jews, Mahometans, and Pagans. By 1896, when Jacobs published his small book on *Barlaam and Josaphat*, the term "world religion" was beginning to gain currency and the list of its members was expanding beyond Christianity and Buddhism. No pagans had been represented at the 1893 meeting of the World's Parliament of Religions in Chicago three years earlier. Yet Jacobs restores Pagans to the list, removes Jews and Muslims, and adds something new: Culture.

In Jacobs's particular version of dualism, Paganism (perhaps reflecting the particular version of Philhellenism of his contemporary, Matthew Arnold) stands on one side, representing life in the world, "the Worship of the Social Bond." The other three religions teach renunciation. There may be any number of reasons for Jacobs's exclusion of Islam from his list of the "four great systems of Religion." As the most recent of the "religions of the book" (Judaism, Christianity, and Islam), perhaps he felt it added nothing new to the perennial question of individual salvation. In his discussion of *Barlaam and Josaphat*, Jacobs discusses the Arabic versions at some length, but traces their elements back to Buddhist sources. The end of the nineteenth century and the last days of the Ottoman empire were yet another chapter in the long European excoriation of Islam.

There may have been different reasons for the exclusion of Judaism from Jacobs's list of world religions. He wrote in a period of pogroms after the assassination of Czar Alexander II in 1881, a time of race theory and of rising anti-Semitism in England. But Jacobs's exclusion of Judaism from "the great systems of Religion" is particularly puzzling because Jacobs was a Jew. Furthermore, he was a founder and president of the Jewish Historical Society of England and he raised funds for Jews in Russia. In 1896, the year of his book on *Barlaam and Josaphat*, he also published the first *Jewish Year Book*, celebrating the accomplishments of British Jews. Yet Judaism is not mentioned as he ends his introduction to *Barlaam and Josaphat*, only Christianity, Buddhism, and Culture. For Jacobs, this last religion is represented by Goethe, when Faust declares:

Too old am I to play with passion;
Too young, to be without desire.
What from the world have I to gain?
Thou shalt abstain—renounce—refrain!
Such is the everlasting song
That in the ears of all men rings,—

That unrelieved, our whole life long,
Each hour, in passing, hoarsely sings.[15]

That "renunciation as the key of salvation is thus the teaching of all modern religions" is a bold claim to make, debatable in the individual cases of Christianity, Buddhism, and even *Faust*. For Jacobs, this teaching must be transmitted through parables for simple folk, and it is to the parables that he attributes the fame of *Barlaam and Josaphat* in the Middle Ages, a time of "lowly minds." Like other nineteenth-century scholars, Jacobs sees medieval people as mired in an ignorance that would be dispelled only by the Renaissance, and he ignores the many philosophers and theologians of the period: a list that might begin with Abelard, Aquinas, and Avicenna.

Regardless of its eccentric conclusion, Jacobs's study of *Barlaam and Josaphat* is an admirable work of scholarship, demonstrating both an impressive knowledge of what was by 1896 a fairly extensive scholarly literature on the topic as well as a discerning eye in its evaluation. For him, "the original work was not intended, or regarded, as specifically religious, or, at any rate, theological. Its teaching is ascetic, it is true, but all religions have a touch of asceticism. It is for the sake of its parables, not for its theology, that the book was taken up, equally by Moslem, Jewish, and Christian writers."[16] He finds evidence for this claim in the Hebrew version, which by his count has ten more parables than any other. It was only in Christianity (he adds "characteristically enough") that the Barlaam story was "surcharged with dogma and turned to polemical uses."[17]

The twentieth century would put *Barlaam and Josaphat* to its own uses while seeking to move closer and closer to its elusive point of origin. In 1981, the Harvard theologian Wilfred Cantwell Smith put *Barlaam and Josaphat* to a rather predictable use in his formulation of what he called "world theology," noting that the story, making its way from Buddhists to Manicheans to Muslims to Christians, had inspired Tolstoy, who wrote about it in his *Confession*. Tolstoy's book had then been read in London by a young Mohandas Gandhi, who would name his community in South Africa "Tolstoy Farm." Gandhi's writings would in turn inspire Martin Luther King Jr.[18]

Still, much of the twentieth-century discourse about *Barlaam and Josaphat* came in the guise of philology. Albert von Le Coq (1860–1930) was the son of a wealthy German wine merchant. After selling the family business in 1900 he volunteered at the Museum of Ethnology in Berlin, where he was eventually assigned to its India section. He was selected to be a member of the Second German Turfan Expedition under the leadership of the distinguished scholar and archaeologist Albert Grünwedel, but when Grünwedel became ill shortly before the expedition was to depart, Le Coq was asked to lead it himself. Le Coq, accompanied by the Pomeranian handyman of the museum and over a ton of luggage, set out in September 1904. Turfan is located in what is today Xinjiang Province of China, then known as Chinese Turkestan. The Silk Road passes through it, and it was home to important Buddhist, Manichean, and Nestorian Christian communities.

The Thousand Buddha Caves at Bezeklik thrived between the eighth and twelfth centuries; they seem to have been abandoned in the sixteenth century when the Uighurs converted to Islam. Le Coq discovered priceless Buddhist frescoes there upon his arrival in 1905. He removed dozens of them, some over ten feet high, from the walls of the caves and transported them to Berlin for their protection; the expedition yielded 103 crates of materials. In the course of the museum's four expeditions, 620 frescoes (many complete, some in fragments) and 290 clay sculptures were removed from various Central Asian sites and taken to Berlin. The Museum of Ethnology was struck by Allied bombs seven times beginning on November 23, 1943, resulting in the destruction of more than half of these artifacts. In addition to the frescoes, Le Coq also returned with many manuscripts, which survived the war. One Old Turkish fragment reads:

> Thereupon the Bodisav Prince drew in the reins of his horse Kaṇṭhaka and halted. Gazing, he asked Chinak: That creature lying there so hideous and groveling, what sort of man is he? Chinak replied, saying respectfully, Your Highness, that man was once a young, healthy, slim, fair youth like yourself. Now he has become old and sick; and since he is afflicted with infirmity, he lies in so hideous a condition. Then the Bodisav spoke thus: Shall we also after a long life finally become dust like this?[19]

Although this passage could simply derive from a Central Asian version of the life of the Buddha, Le Coq and others have identified it as a Manichean text.

According to his biography, Mani was born in Babylonia around 216 CE to a Jewish-Christian father and a Parthian mother. After experiencing visions of a heavenly double, he left for India (in fact, modern Afghanistan), where Buddhism was flourishing. A local king is said to have called him a Buddha. He drew on Christianity, Buddhism, Hinduism, and Zoroastrianism in his teachings and claimed to stand in a lineage of teachers that included Jesus, the Buddha, Krishna, and Zoroaster, whose true teachings he sought to restore to the world. His doctrine was marked by a strict dualism, with good and evil, light and darkness, and the spiritual and material in eternal struggle; practices included fasting, asceticism, and chastity. Manichaeism enjoyed remarkable success, especially between the third and seventh centuries, spreading as far west as Britain (through the Roman legions who were its adherents) and as far east as China.

Some decades after Le Coq, the claim that Manichaeism was central to *Barlaam and Josaphat* would reappear further west. Some of the most famous Christian heretics of the late Middle Ages were the Cathars. This is what others called them; they referred to themselves simply as "good men" (*bons hommes*). They were dualists and believed that there were two gods, a good god of spirit and an evil god of matter. The world, including the body, is the creation of the evil god. They renounced the world, including food that resulted from procreation (and hence were early vegans). They considered themselves Christians, but other Christians considered them heretics because they rejected such important doctrines as virgin birth, physical resurrection, and the sacraments. Among the Cathars, a group called "the pure" renounced marriage and practiced severe asceticism, scorning the opulence and wealth of the Roman Catholic clergy. In 1218, the monk Pierre des Vaux de Cernay described their challenges to Roman Catholic belief:

> They said that almost all the Church of Rome was a den of thieves, and that it was the harlot of which we read in the Apocalypse. They so far annulled the sacraments of the Church, as publicly to teach that the water of baptism was just the same as river water, and that the Host of the most holy body of Christ did not differ from common bread, instilling into the ears of the simple this blasphemy, that the body of Christ, even though it had been as great as the Alps, would have long ago been consumed by those who have eaten of it.[20]

Cathars in southern France were essentially wiped out in a crusade (and subsequent inquisition) ordered by Pope Innocent III in 1208. Few of the Cathars' own texts have survived, and scholars have proposed a range of theories on the origins of their beliefs.

In 1952, the French historian Déodat Roché published a book entitled *Études manichéennes et cathares* in which he examined an Occitan version of *Barlaam and Josaphat* produced in southern France. Noting that Provence had been a Cathar stronghold, he postulated that the story had made its way from the Manicheans to the Cathars, spreading across Europe after their demise. He discerned many Cathar elements in the text. Barlaam is called at one point "*bon homme* Barlaam," monks do not marry and do not eat meat, and the world is based on evil. Those elements of the story that are distinctly contrary to Cathar belief, such as baptism and adoration of the Cross, are for Roché Roman Catholic interpolations made into an original Cathar text that is no longer extant. Scholars have subsequently shown that the elements Roché identified as evidence of Cathar belief are common to most versions of the story, and as Roché himself noted, the values of renunciation, asceticism, and disdain for the world are shared by Buddhists, Muslims, Manicheans, and Christians. The common endorsement of these values explains—at least in part—the broad diffusion of the legend.[21] The story of the Buddha was known to Manicheans, and their religion is renowned for its dualism. Yet this in itself does not seem sufficient evidence to assume that Manichaeism contributed to the theology of *Barlaam and Josaphat*.

In the first half of the twentieth century a great deal of research was published (and contested) on the origins of *Barlaam and Josaphat*, with important contributions from French, German, British, Russian, and Georgian scholars reading texts in a wide range of ancient languages. Rather than reconstruct the rather complicated history of their findings, we summarize the current state of scholarship from their cumulative work.[22]

There has long been agreement that the scores of versions of *Barlaam and Josaphat* in various European languages derive from the Greek text traditionally ascribed to John of Damascus and translated for the first time into Latin in the eleventh century. The traditional attribution of the Greek text to John of Damascus seems to have first been called into question by the French Dominican theologian and historian Michel

Le Quien (1661–1733), and there are many reasons to doubt John's authorship, as we explained in Chapter Four. Subsequent scholarship has shown that the Greek version was translated from a Georgian source and that the translation was once attributed to Euthymius the Iberian (ca. 955–ca. 1024), though it is now considered an anonymous work. The story can be traced back from the many versions in European languages to the Latin, from the Latin to the Greek, from the Greek to the Georgian, from the Georgian to the Arabic, and from the Arabic to the (lost) Persian. A Syriac version as the source of the Persian, postulated by scholars of the late nineteenth century, has never been found and is no longer thought to have existed. The tracing of this line backward in time represents much impressive spadework by generations of impressive scholars. But the trail goes cold here beyond the borders of India, the birthplace of the Buddha.

For David Marshall Lang, translator of both the long and short Georgian versions of *Barlaam and Josaphat*, it is certainly not the case that a Buddhist text was delivered to Jerusalem and then translated into Greek, as the prologue to the Greek text states. He notes cogently that there is likely no single Buddhist text from which the story derives; *Barlaam and Josaphat* is instead "a work in which the ideals of renunciation and the ascetic way of life are woven round certain salient features of the Buddha-elect," with all manner of extraneous parable and fable interpolated along the way.[23] Still, in his brief introduction to his translation of *The Wisdom of Balahvar*, he devotes six pages to passages from a specific Buddhist text, the *Buddhacarita*, passages that sound like passages in *Barlaam and Josaphat*. And he concludes his introduction with these words:

Thus it was that after capturing the imagination of the Manichaeans of Central Asia, the Arabs of Baghdad and the Georgian Christians of the Caucasus, the Bodhisattva attained a fresh incarnation as a holy man of European Christendom. Even though the Middle Ages lacked direct knowledge of the Buddha's teachings, yet his legendary life story contributed to the spiritual formation of the age. That Gautama Buddha was venerated for centuries as a Christian saint, far from providing a theme for sarcasm and scandal, should be regarded as proof of the universal appeal and spiritual virility of the teachings of Śākyamuni.[24]

Lang calls his book *The Wisdom of Balahvar: A Christian Legend of the Buddha*. His translation of the longer Georgian work is titled *The Balavariani: A Buddhist Tale from the Christian East*. In 1986, John C. Hirsh published *Barlam and Iosaphat: A Middle English Life of Buddha*. It is clear that the Buddha no longer looks like Josaphat. Josaphat looks like the Buddha, and since the early twentieth century, Josaphat has largely owed his fame to that resemblance. The Christian prince has been converted to Buddhism.

But *Barlaam and Josaphat*, in any of its myriad iterations, is not a Buddhist story; it is not *the* life, or even *a* life of the Buddha. When the story is considered as a whole, the Buddhist elements of the tale are relatively minor. There are only three: the prophecy, the chariot rides, and the seduction scene, and the seduction scenes are substantially different in the Buddhist and Christian versions. It might even be said that these Buddhist elements function like the many parables added to and subtracted from the various versions of the story. Yet they have become magnified out of any proportion to become the original source of the medieval tale. The presence of these elements has not merely been noted; it is celebrated. It seems that regardless of a scholar's area of expertise—and there are many such areas for *Barlaam and Josaphat*—critical distance seems to dissolve in the presence of the Buddha. How might we account for that?

We recall that at the time the Buddhist origins of *Barlaam and Josaphat* were discovered in Europe, India, Sri Lanka, and Burma were British colonies, and much of Asia was under either direct or indirect European colonial influence. Thomas Rhys Davids, the leading British scholar of Buddhism who wrote at length about the tale, had learned Pali, the sacred Buddhist language of Sri Lanka, while he was a colonial officer there. With colonialism came conversion, or at least attempts at conversion. In centuries past, *Barlaam and Josaphat* returned to Asia and was used by Protestant missionaries in India to convert Hindus and by Jesuit missionaries in Japan to convert Buddhists. In the last half of the twentieth century, many would feel a sense of regret and even shame at the efforts by Christian missionaries, beginning in earnest with Roman Catholics in the sixteenth century and continuing among Catholics and Protestants to the present day, to convert Buddhist cultures to Christianity, a guilt that is apparently felt despite the fact that such efforts have been largely unsuccessful over the centuries. And with that guilt comes a certain schadenfreude that during the entire period that Christians had been condemning Buddhists as idolaters and trying to convert them to Christianity, the Buddha was being celebrated by Catholics on his feast day.

The appeal of Burnouf's Buddha to the modern West is powerful. He was a man who neither claimed to be a prophet of God nor his son, a man who taught a philosophy that seemed to require no dogma, no ritual, and no priests. This view of the Buddha began in Europe in the nineteenth century and persists to the present. In the wake of the critique of Christianity, and especially of Roman Catholicism by the likes of Rousseau and Voltaire—those whom the German theologian Friedrich Schleiermacher would call Christianity's "cultured despisers"—the Buddha was indeed seen as a man of the Enlightenment, an alternative Christ, the teacher of a religion that is not a religion. And so all attempts to convert him to Christianity must be annulled. For the adherent of the religion that we might call liberal humanism, there is a certain pleasure in finding a sage from Asia—so long oppressed, demeaned, and colonized by Europe—at the very heart of the most popular Christian tale of the Middle Ages. In all of its tellings, *Barlaam and Josaphat* was a tale of conquest.

# In Search of the Christian Buddha

When he described Adam's Peak in Sri Lanka, Marco Polo wrote, "And I tell you they say that on this mountain is the sepulchre of Adam our first parent; at least that is what the Saracens say. But the Idolaters say that it is the sepulchre of SAGAMONI BORCAN, before whose time there were no idols." Adam's Peak is likely one of the many places that Marco Polo describes in his book but never saw. If he had climbed to the summit of Adam's Peak, he would have seen a footprint instead of a tomb.

The Portuguese historian Manuel de Faria e Sousa (1590–1649) also never visited the mountain. In fact, he never left Europe, spending most of his life in Madrid. There he worked laboriously on a multivolume history of his compatriots' travels around the world. Three of those were entitled *Ásia Portuguesa*. In the second volume we find the following:

In the Country of *Dinavaca* which is the Center of this
Island rises that vast high Mountain called *Pico de Adam*,
because some believed our first Father lived there, and
that the print of a foot still seen upon a stone on the top
of it, is his; the Natives call it *Amala Saripadi*, that is the
Mountain of the footstep. . . .

The opinion of the Natives is, that *Drama Raja*, Son
of an ancient King of that Island, doing Pennance in that
Mountain with many Disciples, when he was about to
depart at their instance, left that print there as a Memo-
rial; therefore they respect it as a relic of a Saint, and
generally call him *Budam*, that is *Wiseman*.

Some believe this Saint was *Iosaphat*, but it is more
likely it was St. *Thomas*, who has left many Memorials
in the East, and in the West, in *Brasil* and in *Paraguay*.[1]

Our focus is the footprint, but the passage itself requires
some commentary. *Dinavaca* is Denavaka (today spelled Dena-
waka), a region of the island of Sri Lanka. What the Europeans
called Pico de Adam or Adam's Peak is known in Sri Lanka as
Sri Pada or "Glorious Footprint." De Faria reports that it is
also called *amala* or "stainless." The description becomes more
confused in the next paragraph, where he turns to the Buddha.
He calls him *Drama Raja*, a garbled version of *dharmarāja*,
"king of the doctrine," an epithet both of the Buddha and of
pious Buddhist kings. He believed, as many did in his day, that
the Buddha came from Sri Lanka rather than India. In fact,
according to the Buddhist chronicles of Sri Lanka, the Buddha
made three visits from India, the land of his birth, to the island

of Sri Lanka: the first nine months after his enlightenment, the second five years after his enlightenment, and the third nine years after his enlightenment. In each case, he used his magical powers to fly there. As related in the legends of Sri Lanka, when he departed from the island to return to India after his third visit, the Buddha left his footprint on the mountaintop.

De Faria states next that some Europeans believe that the footprint is that of Josaphat. His compatriots' memory of the story may be vague, since the footprint would more likely belong to Barlaam, who, according to some versions of our story, came to India from the island of Sarandib (Sri Lanka). Yet still, de Faria's mention shows that the story of the pious Christian prince continued to circulate in the early modern period. It also shows that centuries after Marco Polo, European travelers continued to carry Josaphat's story to Asia, where the story, or at least elements of the story, had originated a thousand years before.

However, de Faria tells us, the footprint is more likely that of a different saint, not Saint Josaphat but the apostle Thomas, who is said to have taken the Gospel to India to convert the pagans. We have already seen that "India" meant many things to European writers over the centuries and was often conflated with Ethiopia. It apparently also meant the Indies, because in 1549, Manuel da Nóbrega (1517–1570), a Jesuit missionary in Brazil, reported that the local Indians told him that a man named Thum or Zum had brought a kind of root from which they learned to make bread, and that he had also left his footprint in a rock there.

There are footprints all over *Barlaam and Josaphat*, and

much ink has been spilled over the centuries in an effort to determine precisely whose they are. But since the nineteenth century, there has been general agreement that the most important footprints are those of the Buddha. In seventeenth-century Europe, the story of the Buddha looked like the story of Barlaam and Josaphat. In nineteenth-century Europe, *Barlaam and Josaphat* looked like the story of the Buddha. Separated by centuries, European eyes saw similarity. How similar the stories in fact are has been considered in the previous chapters and will be considered again here. It is clear, however, that readers had different motivations for seeing sameness. During the Age of Discovery, European travelers and missionaries were constantly seeking the previous presence of Christianity in distant lands. The mission of many was the conversion of Asia, and they sought signs that they were not the first Christians to set foot in those lands. To identify the footprint on Adam's Peak as that of Josaphat or Saint Thomas, as de Faria did, meant that Asia was not an unknown land and that Western missionaries were following in the footsteps of Christian saints. For others, to find evidence of Christianity confirmed legends of Christian kingdoms flourishing in the East, like that of Prester John. As we saw in Chapter Six, Diogo de Couto went so far as to claim that one of the most famous Buddhist cave-temples in India was the pleasure palace that King Avenir had built for Prince Josaphat. But they were wrong. There never was a King Avenir; there never was a Prince Josaphat; India had never been a Christian land. There had only been the Buddha. The European travelers and missionaries, lacking the tools of modern philology, had misidentified the footprint.

Nineteenth-century scholars also saw sameness, but for different reasons. For Friedrich Max Müller, John of Damascus copied *Barlaam and Josaphat* directly from a Buddhist text laid out on the table before him. For others, Josaphat's servant Zardan was the Buddha's charioteer Chandaka and the sorcerer Theudas was the Buddha's evil cousin Devadatta. For Joseph Jacobs, all the parables were originally Buddhist.

Among the European writers of the nineteenth century, the motivations for seeing sameness also differed. For some, similarities provided evidence of the Aryan origins of the teachings of Jesus. For others, they provided an arena to display the powers of the new science of folkloristics. For yet others, they provided a moment to mock Christians, and especially Roman Catholics, for canonizing an Asian pagan. And for others, similarity offered an ecumenical vision, evidence of a universal religion of humanism, founded not by divine saviors but by human teachers. In each case, European savants armed with the tools of modern philology analyzed the footprint and concluded that it belonged to the Buddha.

## The Buddha and Josaphat

Three prominent elements are commonly cited as tying Josaphat's story to the Buddha's: the prophecy of the prince's future, the chariot scene, and the seduction scene. In earlier chapters we have emphasized that although the stories are similar, they are put to different uses. It may be helpful here to underscore some of those differences. Prophecies of the future of saviors and saints abound in religious literature. Thus, in the story of a pious prince, the prediction that the king's son will reject his earthly kingdom to seek a spiritual realm is not particularly unusual. It is also easy to adapt to a different religious tradition. By contrast, the confinement of the prince in the palace and the chariot rides outside the palace walls are more closely associated with the story of the Buddha's life. But as noted in Chapter One, what scholars regard as the oldest stratum of biographical material in the Buddhist canon contains no reference to the confinement and no reference to the chariot rides. Those elements, so strongly associated with the Buddha, seem to have been added at a later point, centuries after the Buddha's death. Rather than regard those elements as Buddhist in origin, they might be seen as narrative components, admittedly potent components whatever their source, that were inserted into the life of the Buddha long before the story made its way to Persia. These elements eventually became so naturalized that they took on the appearance of an origin story, and were perceived as such by generations of *Barlaam* scholars. The story of the Buddha becomes a source for *Barlaam and Josaphat* only after that story has already been revised and expanded; it would continue to be revised and expanded as it was appropriated into different religious traditions. The Buddhist seduction scene is similarly revised as it is elaborated in the Christian stories. Among the most important differences is that in the Buddhist story, the women of the inner chambers want the prince to revert to the life of conjugal happiness that he knew before he learned of the existence of aging, sickness, and death. In the Muslim and Christian versions, the seductive women want to convert the prince back to his father's idolatrous religion.

Despite the common exaltation of asceticism, the two texts differ fundamentally in doctrine. *Barlaam and Josaphat* is a work fraught with dualism. It is a book of pairs: King Abener and Prince Josaphat, Josaphat and the seducing princess, Barlaam and Josaphat, Nachor and the pagan philosophers, the world and the wilderness, the Body and the Soul. In *Barlaam and Josaphat*, there is no middle way between worldliness and asceticism. In fact, fragments of the story have been found in early collections of Manichean manuscripts. Although the role of Manichaeism in the transmission of the story remains unclear, some scholars have claimed such a role because of the strict opposition between the material world and the spiritual world in *Barlaam and Josaphat*.

In contrast to these strict oppositions, Buddhism is renowned as a middle way between extremes, although Buddhist monasticism might be seen, at least in its textual renditions, as a form of asceticism. However, as the story of the origin of the Buddhist vow of celibacy suggests, the danger in Buddhism is not so much sensuality but "the world," in the sense of family, clan, inheritance, and birthright. The household is the site of suffering, and the goal is not to go to a better world but to put an end to this one. The challenge in Buddhism, then, is not to abstain from the pleasures of this world in order to receive the glories of the world to come; it is not to reject the crown in this world in order to be crowned in heaven. In Buddhism, the goal is simply to acknowledge that the world is inherently flawed by impermanence and death. The goal is to finally stop dying.

The difference between *Barlaam and Josaphat* and Buddhism on this point is clear in the Christian and Buddhist versions of the parable known as "The Herald of Death," discussed in Chapter Two. The king's brother criticizes him for bowing to Christian ascetics dressed in filthy rags: how could the king lower himself before such unworthy men? The king does not respond, but later commands his herald to go and sound the trumpet of death at his brother's door. The king does not execute his brother, but uses his fear to chastise him: "Why then were you astonished at my dismounting and falling down before those who are heralds of Our Lord God and Savior Jesus Christ, who remind me that I shall meet Him face to face, and expound to me the words of his Gospel?"[2]

What scholars like Joseph Jacobs have identified as the Buddhist version of this parable appears in the story of King Aśoka, a historical figure who was a great patron of Buddhism (and in Buddhist accounts, a devout Buddhist) in the third century BCE. Here, the king hears that his brother has criticized him for his patronage of Buddhist monks. He instructs his ministers to tell his brother that when Aśoka is dead, he will become king. It would therefore be wise for him to try on the crown and royal raiment and practice sitting on the throne. The brother reluctantly agrees. The moment he sits on the throne, Aśoka bursts in and accuses his brother of treason. He sentences him to death but, because he is his brother, he gives him a seven-day reprieve, during which time he will be allowed to wear the crown and enjoy all the royal pleasures. On the seventh day Aśoka asks him if he has been enjoying himself, and his brother replies, "Women, dances, songs, palace, beds, seats, youth, beauty, fortune, all that and even the earth with its various jewels have been without charm and empty for me while I saw the executioners in their blue robes sitting tranquilly on their seats at my door."[3]

A single parable may be interpreted in a variety of ways. Elements in the parable may be equated with different realities in different traditions, and the lessons drawn from them may be quite different. In the Christian interpretation of the herald of death parable, God alone decides man's fate and so his heralds are deserving of honor. In the Buddhist story, the fact of death takes all enjoyment from life.

Another parable in *Barlaam and Josaphat* shares elements with this Aśoka story. It recounts the story of a kingdom that has the rather perverse custom of finding an unwitting foreigner each year and making him king. Each new king believes that he will reign until the end of his days and is allowed to rule as he pleases for one year, but at the end of a year the citizens of the city storm the palace, strip him naked, and drive him into another foreign land. At some point, the citizens choose a wise man as their king. When he learns what has happened to those who ruled before him, he transports much of the royal treasury outside the kingdom before the end of the year. Then, when he is deposed and driven out of the country, his treasure awaits him and he lives in comfort for the rest of his life. The Christian moral of the story is clear enough, and it corresponds to the mandate in the Gospel of Matthew to lay up treasures in heaven rather than on earth. The "King for a Year" parable is found in the earliest version of *Barlaam and Josaphat*, the Arabic *Bilawhar and Būdhāsaf*, and the author of this text takes the parable from an Arabic source that may or may not have been influenced by the Buddhist story. Again, the Buddhist and

Christian interpretations of the story are entirely different: the Christian story promises glory after death for all who will accumulate spiritual treasures, whereas in the Buddhist story, the lesson is that all will pass away with death.

Stories of princes renouncing the world abound in Indian literature. In Buddhism, they are found in the biographies of many of the Buddha's disciples, both those from his lifetime and those in subsequent generations. They also occur in stories of the Buddha's past lives, the *jātaka* tales. For example, in one such lifetime the Buddha is born as a prince, and the priests predict his future glory as a king of the four continents. One day, the one-month-old son sits in his father's lap as the king sentences four thieves to various punishments: one will be whipped, one will be imprisoned, one will be struck with a spear, and the last will be impaled. The precocious child is horrified, recalling that in a former life he had been a king for twenty years, after which he was reborn in hell for eighty thousand years. If he succeeds his father, he will be a king again and the sentences he imposes on his subjects will return him to hell at the time of his death. He thus decides to make himself unfit for the throne by pretending to be deaf, dumb, and crippled. He remains in this state for sixteen years, at which point his father, in despair, orders his charioteer to take his son into the forest, dig a hole, kill the boy, and bury him. When they reach the forest, the boy discards his guise and is immediately transformed into a handsome and mighty prince. He proclaims himself an ascetic and tells the charioteer to summon his father. Eventually the king, his sixteen thousand wives, and all the citizens of the kingdom joyfully embrace the ascetic life.[4]

The story sounds something like *Barlaam and Josaphat*. The notion that rule inevitably corrupts the ruler is what motivates the king to divide his kingdom and give half to his pious son. The king reasons that no man can remain pure when he must face the difficult decisions of rule, and that the compromises required of a ruler will lead his son to renounce his renunciation of the world and the worldly. Yet again, a similar story offers very different lessons. In *Barlaam and Josaphat*, the idolatrous king thinks the inevitable duties of a ruler will teach his son that his new religion is false. In the *jātaka* tale, in a former life the Buddha resolves to avoid the worldly entanglements of kingship at all costs, a harbinger of his departure from the palace eons later in his final lifetime.

## Framing Stories

The *jātaka* tales provide yet another perspective on the Buddhist origins of *Barlaam and Josaphat*. Scholars of folklore have been able to trace many of the fables that would become familiar in Europe during the Middle Ages back to India. It is also known that these stories circulated among and were adapted by authors from the various religions of ancient India, including Hinduism, Buddhism, and Jainism. These stories in their Buddhist version (of which there are 547 in a Pali collection) have remained among the most popular forms of Buddhist literature across Asia over the centuries. Dating from the second century BCE, there are some thirty-two *jātaka* stories depicted in stone carvings at the *stūpa* at Bhārhut in India, but only fifteen events from the final life of the Buddha are represented.

Each *jātaka* tale has a frame story. The Buddha is asked a question by someone, and he will say, in effect, "That reminds me of a story." He will then recount a tale in which the protagonist is a noble animal (a monkey, a bird, a fish, a rabbit, an elephant) or a human. At the end of the story, the other side of the frame is provided. The Buddha explains that he was the noble animal or human in that story from one of his past lives, his companions in the tale were his disciples, and his antagonist was, in many cases, his evil cousin Devadatta.

Such a story serves several purposes. First, it provides an opportunity for the Buddha to illustrate his dedication to virtue over lifetimes extending into the ancient past. Second, it provides an opportunity to establish a deep karmic relationship with his disciples; they have been best friends forever. But the *jātakas* are folktales, children's stories, stories that everyone knows. The frame makes the simple tale Buddhist: the rabbit who jumps into a fire to provide a meal for a starving sage becomes the Buddha in a former life. In a sense, the past and all the stories that we tell about it become a stage on which the Buddha always plays the hero. In the *jātaka* tales, not only the past but the imagination itself becomes Buddhist. And so stories circulate as they are told and retold, written and rewritten, put to use to serve a cause—even a cause that claims not to be earthly but spiritual.

As we noted in Chapter Two, the frame tale is also a structure commonly used in early Arab literature, and *Bilawhar and Būdhāsaf* is an example. The Buddha's life story is appropriated and revised into the story of a pious prince and his teacher, and exemplary stories are added to this frame to illustrate the teacher's lessons. A crucial difference from *jātaka* stories is that in the Indian stories, the Buddha teaches; in *Bilawhar and Būdhāsaf* and the Christian *Barlaam and Josaphat*, the Indian prince is the pupil of a wise sage who comes to teach him using parables from Indian and Arabic sources, which he interprets as promoting asceticism.

## Context, Conflict, and Revision

In all the versions of the story, the piety of the prince remains intact, while the king evolves from being kind but concerned in the Buddhist texts to the conflicted king of the Arabic and Christian versions. For the Georgian adapter, the king's persecution of Christians is evil and cruel, and he acts not simply because he hates their religion but because he fears that they will revolt against him and he will lose his throne. In the Greek and Latin translations, the political motivation has been eclipsed by the king's concern for his own religion; in Gui de Cambrai's *Barlaam and Josaphat*, King Avenir's desire to preserve his religion and his kingdom leads him to wage war against his son. In all versions of the story, the king is an idolater, a polemical term used in the Middle Ages to name anyone who practiced a religion other than Christianity, and in many of the vernacular texts, he is called a Saracen. Even as late as the thirteenth century, although some medieval clerics, such as William of Auvergne, grudgingly acknowledged that Muhammad had destroyed idols, others, such as Vincent of Beauvais, proclaimed that Muslims practiced idolatry. The portrayal of Muslims as idolaters was especially common in literary texts and, as we saw in Chapter Five, epic narratives about the battles of Christian Crusaders against Muslims clearly influenced Gui de Cambrai's portrayal of King Avenir and his allies as idolatrous Saracens.

The historical character of the story is not limited to literary history. In *Barlaam and Josaphat*, as may have been the case in medieval Georgia under Muslim rule, the king's court is filled with crypto-Christians: counts, councilors, and retainers hiding their faith while working secretly on its behalf. Unable to overthrow and convert those they perceived to be idolaters, Georgian monks may have relished the defeat and conversion of idolaters in the story they adapted from Arabic. Another Georgian would translate the story into Greek, the sacred language of Christian theology, and adorn it with passages from scripture and from the Church Fathers. For Christians living under Muslim rule, this story, so famous for its parables, is transformed into one long parable itself, one in which the equivalence between the characters in the parable and their parallels in the world, like the faith of the crypto-Christians, remains unspoken.

*Barlaam and Josaphat* thus reflects the contact and conflicts between Muslims and Christians in the Middle Ages, when vast amounts of Islamic learning was translated into Latin, and Christian and Muslim armies went into battle to claim a land they each held holy. This second movement is evoked in the war between King Avenir's Saracen kingdom and Josaphat's Christian lands, described by Gui de Cambrai precisely at the time that the Crusades were taking Christians into Muslim lands. But in Gui's story the positions are reversed: the invader is not the pious Christian but the evil Muslim. The defender is not the evil Muslim but the pious Christian.

India is not to be forgotten in this history, however. Beyond the Buddhist version of the story, beyond the Persian, Arabic, Georgian, Greek, and Latin versions and the scores of vernacular versions that come after that, there is one more version of *Barlaam and Josaphat*: a modern one. That is the story of the prodigious scholarship that has been devoted to the tale over the course of the past century and a half. At the height of its popularity in medieval Europe, there was no question about where *Barlaam and Josaphat* came from. It was the story of two saints that had been recorded by John of Damascus. The story's popularity did not endure, however, whether because of a growing interest in the historicity of saints or because of changing literary tastes. Then, after several centuries of obscurity, *Barlaam and Josaphat* was rediscovered, but not because its readers were interested in sanctity or eternity, or even in Christianity. Modern readers were interested in texts, in the circulation of texts, and in the connections between times and places found in shared literary traditions. Indeed, the modern study of *Barlaam and Josaphat* began when the scholar Theodor Benfey discovered that a Christian tale from medieval Europe, the parable of the man in the well, was also found in a collection of Hindu tales from ancient India.

Once one of the parables from *Barlaam and Josaphat* was traced to India, the connection to the life of the Buddha would soon be proclaimed. From that point, which occurred in the middle of the nineteenth century, the primary attractions of the story have been two. The first is its Buddhist origins, and great effort has been expended by generations of scholars to trace the story back to a precise Buddhist source, thus far with no firm success. The second attraction derives from the rise of the science of philology and the attendant interest in relationships among vernacular versions of *Barlaam and Josaphat*. But in between the quest for origins and the study of differences among the vernacular Christian texts, there is a story of encounter and change: a Buddhist story, perhaps transmitted orally, is appropriated into a Muslim context, and then thoroughly Christianized as the pious prince becomes a saint.

We began with Marco Polo. Let us end with him. Marco Polo described a single grave at the summit of Adam's Peak in Sri Lanka. In fact, it is a single large footprint, set in stone. Buddhists, Muslims, and Christians see the same single large footprint but believe that it comes from different feet. Of his own footprints, the Buddha is reported to have said, "In the future, intelligent beings will see the scriptures and understand. Those of less intelligence will wonder whether the Buddha appeared in the world. In order to remove their doubts, I have set my footprints in stone."[5] The Buddha left his footprints for the benefit of those of us who wonder.

There is much to wonder at, and much to wonder about, in the story we have traced. It is a story about a story. The story began as the life of the Buddha. That life developed over centuries in India, with elements being added along the way. Some of those elements, indeed, some of the most famous of those elements for Buddhists—a prophecy, a chariot ride, an attempted seduction—captivated a Muslim author in Persia during the eighth century just at the time that Muslim armies were beginning to make inroads into northwestern India, where Buddhism flourished. Those armies would play a major role in the demise of Buddhism in India centuries later, and Muslims would condemn Buddhists as idolaters. But the story of the Buddha lived on, unrecognized, in Arabic. In the ninth century, Georgian monks in Jerusalem would take the Muslim story of the Buddha and turn it into a Christian tale at a time when their Georgian homeland suffered under Muslim rule. In the thirteenth century, the story of the Buddha would be told again—by a Jewish translator of the Arabic version and by a Christian writer in France—when French Crusaders were at war with the Muslims over the possession of the holy city of Jerusalem, the very site where Georgian monks had made the story of the Buddha their own three centuries earlier. Three centuries later, Christian missionaries would condemn the Buddha as an idol.

From the perspective of our own age, there is a sad irony in this history. Much blood has been spilled across the centuries in the name of religion, with each proclaiming its truth to be supreme. Over the centuries, four religions saw their truths recounted in a single tale of a pious prince, each unaware of its sources, each unaware of the story's presence in the canon of the others. Each tradition made modifications, and important modifications to be sure, but all tell a version of the same tale. The versions of the legend that becomes *Barlaam and Josaphat* do not teach a single religious truth. What they demonstrate most potently is the power of story itself.

# Acknowledgments

This book was born from a volcano. In April 2010, we were honored to participate in an international conference on *Barlaam and Josaphat* in the Middle Ages held at the University of Vienna, where we met some of the world's leading scholars of the Barlaam legend. On the first day of the conference, a giant ash cloud from the eruption of the volcano in Eyjafjalla-jökull, Iceland, descended on Europe, closing the airports for five days and causing us to extend our stay in Vienna after the conference. It was during long walks through that beautiful city that we decided to write this book, one in which the perspective of a scholar of medieval literature and the perspective of a scholar of Buddhism would be brought together in a single study of this famous tale of a Christian saint. We would therefore like to thank Matthias Meyer and Constanza Cordoni of the University of Vienna for inviting us to the conference.

Back in America, we continued our search for the Christian Buddha, benefiting from the research assistance of Fariba Kanga and Anne Le, and from the advice of test reader Doug Anderson.

# Notes

INTRODUCTION

1   *The Travels of Marco Polo*, trans. Henry Yule, rev. Henri Cordier, 2 vols. (London: John Murray, 1903), 2: 319. Translation modified. All further citations of Marco Polo are from this edition.

2   Ibid., 318. Translation modified.


1. THE STORIED BUDDHA: THE INDIAN TALE

1   The most thorough study of the life of the Buddha remains Hajime Nakamura, *Gotama Buddha: A Biography Based on the Most Reliable Texts*, 2 vols. (Tokyo: Kosei Publishing, 2000, 2005).

2   See Bhikkhu Ñāṇamoli, trans., *The Middle Length Discourses of the Buddha* (Boston: Wisdom Publications, 1995), p. 256.

3   See J. J. Jones, *Mahāvastu*, vol. 2 (London: Luzac & Company, 1952), p. 111.

4   Ibid., p. 113.

5   Ibid., p. 114.

6   See N. A. Jayawickrama, trans., *The Story of Gotama Buddha* (Oxford: The Pali Text Society, 2002), p. 82.

7　See Gwendolyn Bays, trans., *The Voice of the Buddha*, vol. 1 (Berkeley, CA: Dharma Publishing, 1983), pp. 314–15.

8　E. B. Cowell, trans., *The Buddha-Karita of Asvaghosha*, in F. Max Müller, ed., *The Sacred Books of the East*, vol. XLIX, *Buddhist Mahā-yāna Texts* (Oxford: Clarendon Press, 1894), p. 46. We have used this translation because it appeared in the *Sacred Books of the East* series edited by Friedrich Max Müller, who appears in Chapter Seven. This translation would also have been the version available to those who regarded the *Buddhacarita* as the original source of *Barlaam and Josaphat*. For a more recent translation see Patrick Olivelle, trans., *Life of the Buddha by Aśvaghoṣa* (New York: New York University Press and JJC Foundation, 2008).

9　Ibid., p. 58. Translation modified following Olivelle.

10　Jones, *Mahāvastu*, vol. 2, p. 154.

11　See John S. Strong, "A Family Quest: The Buddha, Yaśodharā, and Rāhula in the *Mūlasarvāstivāda Vinaya*," in Julian Schrober, ed., *Sacred Biography in the Buddhist Traditions of South and Southeast Asia* (Honolulu: University of Hawaii Press, 1997), p. 114.

12　Nobuyoshi Yamabe, "*The Sūtra on the Ocean-Like Samādhi of the Visualization of the Buddha*: The Interfusion of the Chinese and Indian Cultures in Central Asia as Reflected in a Fifth Century Apocryphal Sūtra" (Ph.D. dissertation, Yale University, 1999), p. 383.

13　Jones, *Mahāvastu*, vol. 2, p. 154. The language of the original translation has been modernized.

14　See Thanissaro Bhikkhu, trans., *The Buddhist Monastic Code I*, 2nd rev. ed., (Valley Center, CA: Metta Forest Monastery, 2009), p. 13.

15　See Bays, trans., *The Voice of the Buddha*, vol. 1, p. 331.

16　See Bhikkhu Bodhi, trans., *The Connected Discourses of the Buddha*, vol. 2 (Boston: Wisdom Publication, 2000), p. 1844.

17　See Linda Covill, trans., *Handsome Nanda by Aśvaghoṣa* (New York: New York University Press and JJC Foundation, 2007), p. 203.

18　This version appears in a number of sources. See, for example, Marian Ury, *Tales of Times Now Past: Sixty-two Stories from a Medieval Japanese*

*Collection* (Berkeley: University of California Press, 1979), pp. 36 and 37 for a version that appears in the Japanese *Konjaku Monogatarishū*.

## 2. THE BUDDHA BECOMES A PROPHET: THE ARABIC *BILAWHAR AND BŪDHĀSAF*

1 Valerie Hansen, *The Silk Road: A New History* (Oxford: Oxford University Press, 2012), p. 5.

2 François de Blois, "On the Sources of the Barlaam Romance, or: How the Buddha Became a Christian Saint," *Literarische Stoffe und ihre Gestaltung in mitteliranischer Zeit: Kolloquium anlässlich des 70. Geburtstages von Werner Sundermann*, ed. Desmond Durkin-Meisterernst, Christiane Reck and Dieter Weber (Wiesbaden: Ludwig Reichert Verlag, 2009), pp. 18–19.

3 Tarif Khalidi, *Arabic Historical Thought in the Classical Period* (Cambridge: Cambridge University Press, 1994), pp. 92–93.

4 Dimitri Gutas, "Classical Arabic Wisdom Literature: Nature and Scope," *Journal of the American Oriental Society* 101, no. 1 (1981): 59–61; Daniel Gimaret, *Le livre de Bilawhar et Būḏāsf selon la version arabe ismaélienne* (Geneva: Droz, 1971), pp. 38–40.

5 For information on the manuscripts, see Gimaret's French translation, *Le livre de Bilawhar et Būḏāsf*, pp. 9–10, and his edition of the text, *Kitāb Bilawhar wa Būḏāsf* (Beirut: Dar al-Mashraq, 1972), pp. 11–20; see also De Blois, "On the Sources of the Barlaam Romance," p. 7.

6 De Blois, "On the Sources of the Barlaam Romance," p. 9. See pp. 10–12 for a schematic comparison of the two versions. See also François de Blois, *Arabic, Persian, and Gujarati Manuscripts: The Hamdani Collection in the Library of the Institute for Islamic Studies* (London: Tauris, 2011), pp. 189–90.

7 Gimaret, *Le livre de Bilawhar et Būḏāsf*, pp. 31–32.

8 All citations of *Bilawhar and Būdhāsaf* are translated by the authors from the French of Daniel Gimaret, *Le livre de Bilawhar et Būḏāsf*.

9 Daniel Gimaret, "Bouddha et les bouddhistes dans la tradition musulmane," *Journal Asiatique* 257 (1969): 282.

10  On Islamic knowledge of Buddhism, see Gimaret, "Bouddha et les bouddhistes," 277–78. The rest of this section is closely based on Gimaret's account.

11  Ibid., pp. 273–74.

12  Ibid., pp. 276–77.

13  See Bruce B. Lawrence, *Shahrastānī on Indian Religions* (The Hague: Mouton, 1976), p. 42. For a discussion of this passage and other Islamic references to the Buddha, see pp. 110–14 of the same volume.

14  Gimaret, "Bouddha et les bouddhistes," 280; our translation from Gimaret's translation into French.

15  Ibid., pp. 279–82.

16  Ibid., p. 282.

17  We discuss the longer version of *Bilawhar and Būdhāsaf*, available in Gimaret's modern French translation.

18  De Blois, "On the Sources of the Barlaam Romance," p. 14.

19  Gimaret, *Bilawhar et Būḏāsf*, pp. 15–17.

20  De Blois, "On the Sources of the Barlaam Romance," p. 17.

### 3. THE PRINCE BECOMES A CHRISTIAN SAINT: THE GEORGIAN *BALAVARIANI*

1  Joseph Patrich, *Sabas, Leader of Palestinean Monasticism: A Comparative Study in Eastern Monasticism, Fourth to Seventh Centuries* (Washington, D.C.: Dumbarton Oaks, 1995), p. 8.

2  Archpriest Zakaria Machitadze, *Lives of the Georgian Saints*, trans. from the Georgian by David and Lauren Elizabeth Ninoshvili (Platina, CA: St. Herman of Alaska Brotherhood, 2006), pp. 359–60.

3  David Marshall Lang, *The Balavariani: A Tale from the Christian East Translated from the Old Georgian* (Berkeley and Los Angeles: University of California Press, 1966), p. 69. All citations of the *Balavariani* are from this translation.

4  Daniel Gimaret, "Traces et parallèles du *Kitāb Bilawhar wa Būḏāsf* dans la tradition arabe," *Bulletin des études orientales* 24 (1971): 111–17.

5  François de Blois, "On the Sources of the Barlaam Romance, or: How

the Buddha Became a Christian Saint," *Literarische Stoffe und ihre Gestaltung in mitteliranischer Zeit: Kolloquium anlässlich des 70. Geburtstages von Werner Sundermann*, ed. Desmond Durkin-Meisterernst, Christiane Reck and Dieter Weber (Wiesbaden: Ludwig Reichert Verlag, 2009), pp. 15–16. However, Daniel Gimaret argues that *Bilawhar and Būdhāsaf* is the original version of the parable in "Traces et parallèles," pp. 117–21.

6 Lang, *The Balavariani*, pp. 48–49.

## 4. THE SAINT IS TRANSLATED: GREEK AND LATIN VERSIONS OF THE *BARLAAM* LEGEND

1 Translation slightly modified for context. All English translations from the Greek are from *Barlaam and Ioasaph*, trans. G. R. Woodward and H. Mattingly (Cambridge, MA: Harvard University Press, 1914); they have been modified throughout to modernize spelling and syntax.

2 On the persistent conflation of India and Ethiopia in the Middle Ages, see Mary Baine Campbell, "Asia, Africa, Abyssinia: Writing the Land of Prester John," in *Travel Writing, Form, and Empire: The Poetics and Politics of Mobility*, ed. Julia Kuehn and Paul Smethurst (New York: Routledge, 2009).

3 See John Block Friedman, *The Monstrous Races in Medieval Art and Thought* (Cambridge, MA: Harvard University Press, 1981; reprint, Syracuse: Syracuse University Press, 2000).

4 Ilia V. Abuladze, "Introduction," in David Marshall Lang, *The Balavariani* (Berkeley: University of California Press, 1966), p. 41.

5 On the history and diffusion of the Latin translations, see the recent edition by Óscar de la Cruz Palma, *Barlaam et Iosaphat: Versión vulgata latina, con la traducción del latín de Juan de Arce Solorceno* (Madrid: Consejo Superior de Investigaciones Científicas, 2001).

6 For an introduction to medieval hagiography, see Thomas Head, ed., *Medieval Hagiography: An Anthology* (New York: Routledge, 2001).

7 Alain Boureau, *La légende dorée: Le système narratif de Jacques de Voragine* (Paris: Cerf, 1984), pp. 21–25.

8 Sherry L. Reames, *The* Legenda Aurea: *A Reexamination of Its Paradoxical History* (Madison: University of Wisconsin Press, 1985).

9 Jacobus de Voragine, *The Golden Legend: Readings on the Saints*, trans. William Granger Ryan, 2 vols. (Princeton, NJ: Princeton University Press, 1993). All citations of *The Golden Legend* are from this translation.

10 It was well known in Arab literary sources; see Daniel Gimaret, "Traces et parallèles du *Kitāb Bilawhar wa Būḏāsf* dans la tradition arabe," *Bulletin des études orientales* 24 (1971): 129–30.

11 De Voragine, *The Golden Legend*, pp. xvi–xviii.

### 5. THE PIOUS PRINCE GOES TO WAR: GUI DE CAMBRAI'S *BARLAAM AND JOSAPHAT*

1 David Marshall Lang, *The Balavariani: A Tale from the Christian East translated from the Old Georgian* (Berkeley and Los Angeles: University of California Press, 1966), p. 125.

2 Gui de Cambrai, *Balaham und Josaphas: Nach den Handschriften von Paris und Monte Cassino*, ed. Carl Appel (Halle: Niemeyer, 1907). See also *Barlaam and Josaphat: A Christian Tale of the Buddha*, trans. Peggy McCracken (New York: Penguin, 2014). All citations are from this translation.

3 Gui de Cambrai, *Le vengement Alixandre*, in *Elliott Monographs*, no. 25, ed. Bateman Edwards (Princeton, NJ: Princeton University Press, 1928).

4 On the Arabic versions of this story, see Daniel Gimaret, "Traces et parallèles du *Kitāb Bilawhar wa Būḏāsf* dans la tradition arabe," *Bulletin des études orientales* 24 (1971): 121–29.

5 For a history of the Crusades see Jonathan Riley-Smith's *The Crusades: A Short History* (New Haven, CT: Yale University Press, 1987).

6 Charles Manekin, ed., *Medieval Jewish Philosophical Writings*, Cambridge Texts in the History of Philosophy (Cambridge, UK: Cambridge University Press, 2008), p. ix.

7 Abraham ibn Ḥasdāy, *Ben ham-melekh we-han-haẓir*, ed. Abraham Meir Haberman (Tel Aviv, Israel: Mahbārōt le-Sifrût, 1950); translation into

Catalan by Tessa Calders i Arýís, *El Princep i el Monjo, D'Abraham ben Semuel ha-Levi ibn Ḥasdāy* (Sabadell, Spain: Editorial AUSA, 1987).

8    The description of the Hebrew text comes from Daniel Gimaret, trans., *Le livre de Bilawhar and Būḏāsf selon la version arabe ismaélienne* (Geneva, Switzerland: Droz, 1971), pp. 48–50.

## 6. THE BUDDHA BECOMES JOSAPHAT: EARLY MODERN READERS

1    Giovanna Frosini, "Il principe et l'eremita. Sulla tradizione dei testi italiani della storia di 'Barlaam e Iosafas,'" *Studi medievali*, 3rd series, no. 1 (1996): 1–63.

2    Cited in A. C. Moule and Paul Pelliot, eds. and trans., *The Description of the World*, vol. 1 (London: George Routledge & Sons, 1938), p. 140.

3    Emmanuel Cosquin, "La légende des saints Barlaam et Josaphat: son origine," *Revue des questions historiques* 28 (1880): 579–600, especially p. 580.

4    Pierre Daniel Huet, Bishop of Avranches, *De l'origine des romans*, 2nd ed. (1678), p. 87, cited in Cosquin, "La légende," p. 587.

5    *Martyrologe universel* (Paris: 1709), cited in Cosquin, "La légende," p. 589.

6    Cosquin, "La légende," p. 589.

7    Ibid., pp. 586–600.

8    Francis Xavier, *The Letters and Instructions of Francis Xavier*, translated and introduced by M. Joseph Costelloe, S. J. (St. Louis, MO: Institute of Jesuit Sources, 1992), pp. 336–37. Letter "To His Companions in Europe" from Cochin [Kochi], January 29, 1552.

9    For a study of the Japanese version, see Keiko Ikegami, *Barlaam and Josaphat: A Transcription of MS Egerton 876 with Notes, Glossary, and Comparative Study of the Middle English and Japanese Versions* (New York: AMS Press, 1999).

10   Athanasius Kircher, *China Illustrata*, trans. Charles D. Van Tuyl (Bloomington: Indiana University Research Institute, 1987), p. 123.

11   Ibid., pp. 141–42.

12   Louis le Comte, *Memoirs and Observations Topographical, Physical,*

*Mathematical, Mechanical, Natural, Civil, and Ecclesiastical Made in a Late Journey through the Empire of China, and Published in Several Letters. Particularly upon the Chinese Pottery and Varnishing; the Silk and Other Manufactures. Description of their Cities and Publick Works; Number of People, their Language, Manners and Commerce; their Oeconomy, and Government. The Philosophy of Confucius. The State of Christianity, with Many Other Curious and Useful Remarks*, trans. from the Paris edition (London, 1697), pp. 323, 325.

13  This passage has been adapted from *The Travels of Marco Polo: The Complete Yule-Cordier Edition*, vol. 2 (New York: Dover Publications, 1992), p. 325. Henry Yule adds a number of ellipses in this quotation. These have been restored from the original Portuguese with the assistance of Juan Udaondo Alegre.

14  Cited in Cardinal Henri de Lubac, *La rencontre du bouddhisme et de l'Occident* (Paris: Le Éditions du Cerf, 2000), p. 29.

15  Cited in *The Travels of Marco Polo*, p. 325.

### 7. JOSAPHAT BECOMES THE BUDDHA: MODERN READERS

1  *The Life and Letters of the Right Honourable Friedrich Max Müller, Edited by His Wife*, 2 vols. (London: Longmans, Green, and Co., 1902), vol. 1, p. 34.

2  Eugène Burnouf, *Introduction to the History of Indian Buddhism*, trans. Katia Buffetrille and Donald S. Lopez Jr. (Chicago, IL: University of Chicago Press, 2009), p. 159.

3  Ibid., p. 329.

4  Hermann Oldenberg, *Buddha: His Life, His Doctrine, His Order*, trans. William Hoey (London: Williams and Norgate, 1882), p. 1.

5  Theodor Benfey, *Pantschatantra: Fünf Bücher indischer Fabeln, Märchen, und Erzählungen*, vol. 1 (Leipzig: F. A. Brockhaus, 1859), pp. 82–83.

6  Laboulaye wrote a two-part review of Stanislas Julien's three-volume translation from the Chinese, *Les Avadânas*. Both parts appeared under the title "Variétés," the first on July 21, 1859 (page 3, column 2), the sec-

ond on July 26, 1859 (beginning on page 2, column 5). The discussion of *Barlaam and Josaphat* occurs on page 3, columns 3–4 of the July 26 edition.

7   Felix Liebrecht, "Die Quellen des 'Barlaam und Josaphat,'" *Jahrbuch für romanische und englische Sprach und Literatur* 2 (1860): 314.

8   Philippe Édouard Foucaux, *Rgya tch'er rol pa; ou Développment des jeux, contenant l'histoire du Bouddha Çakya-Mouni traduit sur la version tibétaine du Bkah hgyour, et revu sur l'original sanscrit (Lalitavistâra)* (Paris: L'Imprimerie royale, 1847–1848). He would publish a translation of the same text from the Sanskrit in the *Annales du Musée Guimet* (1887–1892).

9   F. Max Müller, *Chips from a German Workshop*, vol. 4: *Essays Chiefly on the Science of Language* (London: Longmans, Green, and Co., 1875), pp. 175–76, n. 3.

10  Ibid., pp. 188–89. For a slightly different version, see Friedrich Max Müller, *Selected Essays on Language, Mythology and Religion*, vol. 1 (London: Longmans, Green, and Co., 1881), pp. 546–47.

11  Thomas W. Rhys Davids, *Buddhist Birth-Stories* (London: George Routledge and Sons Ltd, 1880), p. xlvi.

12  K. S. MacDonald, *The Story of Barlaam and Joasaph: Buddhism & Christianity* (Calcutta: Thacker, Spink & Co., 1895), p. ii.

13  Joseph Jacobs, *Barlaam and Josaphat: English Lives of Buddha* (London: David Nutt, 1896), p. xi.

14  Ibid., p. xciv–xcv.

15  Johann Wolfgang von Goethe, *Faust: A Tragedy*, First Part, trans. Bayard Taylor (London: Strahan & Co. Publishers, 1871), p. 75.

16  Jacobs, *Barlaam and Josaphat*, p. xl.

17  Ibid., p. xli.

18  Wilfred Cantwell Smith, *Toward a World Theology: Faith and the Comparative History of Religion* (London: Macmillan, 1981), pp. 7–11.

19  Cited in David Marshall Lang, *The Wisdom of Balahvar: A Christian Legend of the Buddha* (London: George Allen and Unwin, 1957), p. 27.

20  See Edward Peters, ed., *Heresy and Authority in Medieval Europe: Doc-*

*uments in Translation* (Philadelphia: University of Pennsylvania Press, 1980), p. 124.

21   Monique Bonnier Pitts, *Barlam et Joʒaphas: Roman du XIVe siècle en langue d'Oc* (Paris: Presses de l'Université de Paris, 1989), p. 239.

22   This summary is drawn largely from the work of David Marshall Lang, the leading scholar of the Georgian versions of the tale, especially his *The Wisdom of Balahvar: A Christian Legend of the Buddha* (London: George Allen and Unwin, 1957) and his *The Balavariani* (Berkeley: University of California Press, 1966). The highly informative introduction to the latter work is by the Georgian scholar Ilia V. Abuladze.

23   Lang, *The Wisdom of Balahvar*, pp. 12–13.

24   Ibid., p. 64.

CONCLUSION

1   Manuel de Faria e Sousa (or Manoel Faria y Souza), *The Portugues Asia, or, The History of the Discovery and Conquest of India by the Portugues Containing All Their Discoveries from the Coast of Africk, to the Farthest Parts of China and Japan, All Their Battels by Sea and Land, Sieges and Other Memorable Actions, A Description of Those Countries, and Many Particulars of the Religion, Government and Customs of the Natives*, trans. Capt. John Stevens (London: 1695), pp. 509–10.

2   See David Marshall Lang, *The Wisdom of Balahvar: A Christian Legend of the Buddha* (London: George Allen and Unwin, 1957), p. 75.

3   Eugène Burnouf, *Introduction to the History of Indian Buddhism*, trans. Katia Buffetrille and Donald S. Lopez Jr. (Chicago, IL: University of Chicago Press, 2009), p. 393.

4   In the Pali collection, this is the *Mūga-pakkha Jātaka*.

5   See George Roerich, *Biography of Dharmasvāmin (Chag lo tsa-ba Chos-rje-dpal), A Tibetan Monk Pilgrim* (Patna, India: K. P. Jayaswal Research Institute, 1959), p. 17. Roerich's translation is mistaken and has been corrected here.

# Index